THE INVISIBLE WEAPON

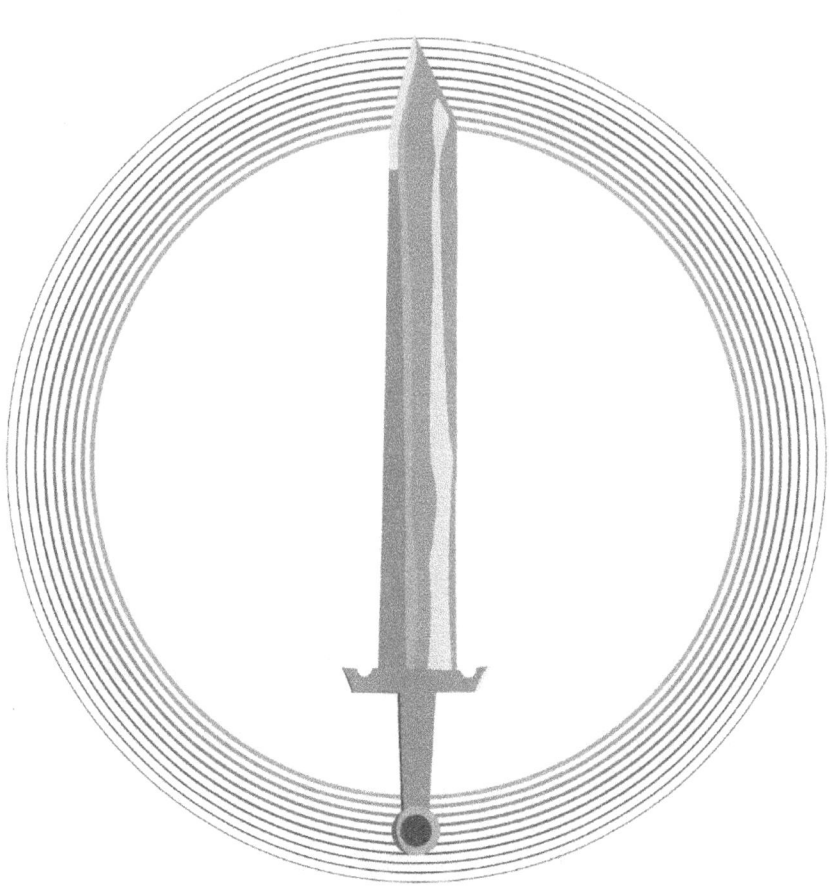

GEORGE RIVERS

The Invisible Weapon

The College Athlete's Most Valuable Asset

HEARTS & MINDS

This book is designed to provide information that the author believes to be accurate on the subject matter it covers and is written from the author's personal experience. In the text that follows, many people's and company's names and identifying characteristics have been changed, so that any resemblance to actual persons, living or dead, events, companies or locales is entirely coincidental.

Any references to resources and materials produced by other entities are purely the author's own interpretation. The author does not imply an endorsement from any of the sources cited within this book.

ISBN 978-1-7339954-3-6 (paperback)

The Invisible Weapon: The College Athlete's Most Valuable Asset

Copyright © 2023 by Hearts & Minds.

All rights reserved. Neither this book, nor any part of this book, either print or electronic, may be used or reproduced in any form or by any means without the express permission of the author, except for the use of brief quotations in a book review. Failure to comply with these terms may expose you to legal action and damages, including copyright infringement.

First Printing, 2023

Hearts & Minds

Acknowledgements

First and foremost I would like to give thanks and praise to my Lord and Savior Jesus Christ for giving me the opportunity to write this book and give me the platform to make a difference in the world through Him. Without my faith none of this would be possible.

I would like to thank my parents, friends, and coaches along the way who have helped me become the man that I am today, the ones who believed in me during the tough times, who picked me up when I was down, and instilled in me to always keep moving forward. You know who you are and you will always have a special place in my heart.

A huge thank you to my copy editor Kathy and my book designer Jacob, you guys knocked it out of the park with your hard work and dedication.

I would also like to thank Trevor Conner, CEO of Hearts & Minds for believing in me and welcoming me with open arms to the team. Without his faith, leadership, and passion for helping people, this book would not exist.

Proverbs 27:17

Table of Contents

Chapter One
Introduction to Mental Training — 1

Chapter Two
Mental Toughness — 12

Chapter Three
Athlete Resilience — 23

Chapter Four
Motivation — 39

Chapter Five
Concentration & Focus — 54

Chapter Six
Sport Confidence — 74

Chapter Seven
Accountability — 90

Chapter Eight
Goal Setting — 112

Chapter Nine
Performance Anxiety — 126

Chapter Ten
Mental Health & Recovery — 142

About The Author — 147

Chapter One: Introduction to Mental Training

HAVING WALKED IN YOUR SHOES, I've competed at both the junior and collegiate levels, navigating through numerous highs and lows throughout my career. I've faced season-ending injuries, endured mental collapses, and weathered the storms of heartbreaks and successes. I've witnessed the spectrum of positives and pitfalls natural in college athletics, experiencing firsthand the daily struggles that college athletes confront.

Competing in college can be incredibly rewarding, but it also presents significant challenges. I've lived this as an athlete and observed it from the sidelines as a coach. Over four years of college competition and seven years of coaching at the collegiate level, I've come to realize that the most significant differentiator between the good and the great is the mind. The mentally tough athletes seem to have it all figured out, and the reality is, they do – MENTALLY.

This book aims to provide you with the tools, guidance, and a pathway to transform your mind into a powerful weapon. Are you interested? Do you want that edge? If so, read on.

The phrase, "the complete player" is often thrown around in the sports world. Tune into any radio show, tv interview, or social media post and you will see examples of how so and so is "complete" or "they have it all." But, what does that really mean? Does it mean they have the perfect technique, superior physical strength, or off the charts athleticism? Absolutely, all of those characteristics can define "the complete player." As humans, we are naturally drawn to visual and concrete results, evaluating athletes based on their accomplishments and physical presence. Yet, a crucial element in what makes a player "complete" goes beyond the physical results. The missing puzzle piece that makes an athlete great and "complete" is their mental game. This is the driving force behind their physical prowess and can differentiate whether one is a good or great athlete. Mental toughness is the key ingredient that allows an athlete to reach their highest potential; to be able to perform on a consistent basis no matter what obstacles stand in their way.

Understanding and mastering the mental game gives athletes an extra edge. It enables them to maintain focus during competitions and make intelligent decisions – both physically and tactically – regardless of the circumstances they encounter in the heat of the moment. It requires immense discipline and determination to remain focused and perform at a high level under pressure. This discipline and focus are what distinguishes the good athletes from the great ones. They don't let distractions or doubts get in their way of achieving success. Mentally strong athletes have an edge that cannot be bought with any amount of money – it can only be trained. It is solely up to you, the athlete, to take charge, to commit, and build your mind as you would your body. In reality, the mind controls the body, not the other way around.

Before you continue, take a moment and reflect on both your past and present. Ask yourself these questions:
- What is missing in my game?
- What is holding me back from being a great athlete and competitor?
- Why are others reaching the next level and I am not?

These are very important questions to consider as you plan for future competition. Perhaps you have come to the idea that you are not as complete of a player as you want to be. You may also believe that you are missing that edge that could set you apart from others. If that's you, read on!

Throughout this book you will be given the mental weapons to take your game to the next level and sharpen your most important weapon: your mind.

Mental Training

Mental training is described as "the process of developing cognitive skills and mental resilience through various techniques and exercises that leads to increased sports performance". The English definition is, "Mental skills training in sports is like going to the gym, but for your mind...you learn how to build your mind as you would your body." Mental training is not rocket science. True, there are numerous academic papers, an abundance of books, and even courses taught at the master's and doctoral levels. The same can be said for physical training, yet it is more widely accepted and not perceived as a complex science. However, when it comes to the mind, people often feel intimidated. The human mind is the most complex subject ever studied; we still lack a complete understanding of the mind compared to what we know about our bodies. Unlike the body, the mind knows no boundaries; it is always active and is the primary decision-maker in all aspects of life, including sports. This fact alone should motivate you to develop the mental skills to harness the mind's power and gain a competitive edge to triumph over opponents.

    Mental skills training and development are crucial components for success in all aspects of life. This training enables individuals to effectively deal with challenges and difficult circumstances, fostering the ability to manage emotions and maintain focus on the task at hand. Strengthening mental resilience enhances better decision-making abilities and equips individuals to solve problems more effectively, even under pressure. Improved mental strength facilitates adaptation to stressful situations, which can lead to increased productivity. Furthermore, it instills resilience in the face of failure by teaching individuals to respond positively and adjust quickly during challenging times. Developing strong mental skills cultivates confidence and competence in dealing with various situations, ranging from stressful personal relationships to large-scale business projects.

Mental strength training establishes a cornerstone for success both in and out of the sports world, enabling a deeper self-understanding, fortified self-discipline, and development of an inner source of motivation. This training enhances cognitive clarity, improves communication skills, and facilitates the setting of well-defined goals. Additionally, it equips individuals to be able to manage stress in a healthy manner while effectively adapting to change. Essential to the pursuit of enduring success and happiness, mental strength training proves invaluable not only in the sports world but also in the broader game of life.

Common Misperceptions about Mental Skills Training

Now, let's discuss what mental training isn't. It's not about sitting in a dimly lit room, casually sharing feelings while a therapist jots down notes – a stereotype often portrayed in movies and TV shows. Contrary to the common misconception that it solely involves "talking it out" and "analyzing your feelings", mental training transcends these ideas. It encompasses a proactive approach to enhance one's well-being, much like how one strategically improves in areas like physical fitness or nutrition. It involves a proactive approach to improvement rather than the reactionary solution to a specific problem. Consider it similar to going to the gym; you wouldn't cease working out once you have achieved stronger biceps. The same principle applies to mental training, emphasizing continuous growth and development.

It is crucial to address the unique stigma surrounding mental skills training in the athletic world. Imagine a teammate approaching you after practice, revealing they are working with a mental coach or reading a sports psych book. What would your initial reaction be? Would it be curiosity and a desire to learn more, or would it lean toward the assumption that something must be wrong with them, interpreting seeking help for mental aspects as a sign of weakness? If your first thought aligns with the latter, it's not uncommon, it reflects the prevailing perception of mental training and mental health services in general. There are three primary stigmas attached to mental training in sport. The first involves social misunderstandings, where there is a misconception that only those with "serious problems" require psychological help, creating an unnecessary barrier for athletes who could benefit from these services. The second revolves around the perception of weakness; athletes, especially in elite circles, are often expected to show only mental toughness. Seeking help for mental challenges may be viewed as a sign of weakness, dissuading athletes from seeking assistance. The third stigma involves stereotypes, often depicted in movies – sitting on a couch and talking about feelings, which isn't reality. Consider the irony; you're holding a book right now, challenging these stereotypes. This highlights the problem, explaining why athletes might shy away from mental training services, books, or other resources in their quest for answers to improve their performance. It's worth recognizing that by engaging with this book, you already possess an advantage over many athletes who avoid it due to the prevailing stigmas surrounding mental training. It is also important to address the stigma surrounding mental skills training that is unique in the athletic world.

Importance of Mental Training

"Sports is a game of chess, not checkers, "is a familiar saying we've all heard, and one that highlights the complex nature of athletic competition. Playing a sport is more than just "competing hard"; it involves multiple factors contributing to winning a game or a match. Prior to competition, careful planning, strategy development, and preparation for the unknown are essential. Throughout the actual competition, athletes engage in a continuous process of making thousands, if not millions, of split-second decisions. This demands constant analysis, prediction of opponents' moves, and finding solutions to unforeseen challenges in the pursuit of victory.

The mind is in a perpetual state of activity before, during and after competition. Unsurprisingly, the most successful athletes hone their mental skills to enhance their overall performance and achieve success.

When two opponents are evenly matched in terms of physical abilities, the differentiating factor becomes evident – the mind! The body isn't responsible for handling factors such as confidence, emotional control/stability, motivation, concentration, and focus; it's the mind that governs these aspects, ultimately determining the outcome of the competition. When athletes are evenly matched in physical abilities, success in sports hinges on how sharp they are mentally. Keep in mind, there is truth to the saying "sports is like a game of chess, not checkers," where the mind plays the decisive role in determining the ultimate victor.

Success and Mental Training

The study "The Role of Sport Psychology in Enhancing Athlete Performance" conducted by Smith et al.[1], delves into the impact of sports psychology themes on athlete performance. The research reveals that techniques like goal-setting and self-talk, skills covered in this book, significantly enhance athletic performance across various sports. Importantly, the study emphasizes that improving mental skills and strategies is as crucial as physical strength and conditioning for success in sports. This underscores the importance of developing mental skills to maximize performance. As an athlete, it's crucial to explore and utilize every available tool to reach your peak performance level.

Another relevant study, "Exploring the Effects of Psychological Skills Training on Athletes' Performance Levels" by Baker Côté, and Abernethy[2], explores how practicing psychological

---

[1] Smith, et al. "The Role of Sport Psychology in Enhancing Athlete Performance". In:International Journal of Sport and Exercise Psychology 1.3 (2003): 307-324.
[2] [^2]: Côté, Baker, and Abernethy. "Exploring the Effects of Psychological Skills Training on Athletes' Performance Levels". In: Journal of Applied Sport Psychology 1.1 (2003): 45-60.

skills training (PST), also known as mental skills training, influences how well athletes perform. The research suggests that incorporating PST into an athlete's routine can result in enhancements in concentration, confidence, and stress management, contributing to an overall improvement in performance. These themes are central to our discussion in this book. Athletes must capitalize on the accessible mental tools to optimize their performance. As evident from the mentioned studies, engaging in mental skills training is vital for your growth as an athlete and extends beyond the realm of sports. The topics covered in this book are designed to benefit you not only in enhancing your performance in your chosen sport but also in various aspects of life.

Mental Toughness Self-Assessment

Before you continue, your journey to develop mental strength as an athlete begins right NOW! Take a few minutes to honestly evaluate yourself. This self-assessment will serve as a benchmark for tracking your mental progress throughout the book. Rate your responses on a scale of 1 to 10, where 1 represents a poor rating and 10 signifies excellence.

INSTRUCTIONS: On the following page, please complete the self – assessment.

Self-Evaluation

1. **Attitude:** Do you maintain a positive attitude on the field or court?
2. **Concentration/Focus:** Are you easily distracted during practice or competition, or can you maintain laser focus?
3. **Effort:** Do you consistently give 100% in both practice and competition, regardless of the circumstances?
4. **Discipline:** Are you well-prepared for practices and competitions, consistently on time, and committed to daily tasks?
5. **Body Language:** Does your outward appearance on the field or court exude confidence, making it difficult for opponents and fans to discern whether you are winning or losing?
6. **Self-Talk:** Is your inner dialogue predominantly positive, free from being burdened by negative thoughts and potential outcomes?
7. **Emotional Control:** When faced with challenging situations, do you react positively and prevent your emotions from taking control or hindering productive and clear thinking?
8. **Motivation**: Are you driven daily to achieve your goals, unafraid of taking on new challenges?
9. **Confidence:** Do you genuinely believe in yourself, confident that you can achieve significant accomplishments in your sport and life, equipped with the necessary tools?
10. **Goal Setting:** Do you regularly set small and long-term achievable goals that provide a sense of accomplishment upon attainment?

Once you have finished this self-assessment, hold onto it. Regularly revisit it and use it as a tool to gauge your mental progress as you acquire and apply new skills in your daily life, practice, and competitions. Reflecting on and acknowledging your progress is a valuable mental skill that will contribute significantly to your overall personal and athletic development.

Chapter Two: Mental Toughness

In the realm of sports, we all aspire to attain that elusive quality: mental toughness. But what does that really mean? What factors contribute to its makeup and what qualities contribute to the development of mental toughness?

Mental toughness, at its core, is the ability to manage the challenges that will surely come our way during our journey, ensuring they do not hinder our pursuit of success on the field or court. It goes beyond just skill; it involves developing the ability to concentrate on the process rather than fixate on the end result. This skill includes staying positive in the face of adversity. While mental toughness can be developed through consistent practice, unwavering dedication, and hard work, it demands more than just sheer physical effort to build its foundation.

To excel as an athlete, it is crucial to develop the correct mindset – one that allows you to overcome challenges, maintain focus on your goals, and effectively utilize available resources. Mental toughness involves seizing command of your thoughts, emotions and energy, enabling peak performance when it matters most. Doesn't that sound like an ideal scenario? Certainly, mental toughness is what sets athletes apart, taking them from being just good to truly great!

What Mental Toughness Is Not

To truly understand mental toughness, let's clear up what it isn't. Athletes who struggle with mental toughness frequently find themselves grappling with persistent challenges throughout their careers.

- **Struggle with Focus:**
    - Difficulty maintaining concentration during both practice and games.
    - Easily distracted by external factors or activities in their surroundings.
- **Inconsistent Performance:**
    - Display inconsistency in performance, often linked to low motivation levels.
- **Pressure Distractions:**

- ○ Prone to distraction, particularly in high-pressure moments, diverting attention away from the present situation.
- **Handling Criticism:**
  - ○ Difficulty coping with criticism or feedback from coaches, parents, or teammates.
  - ○ Personal attachment to feedback rather than utilizing feedback constructively.
- **Avoidance of Challenges:**
  - ○ Tendency to give up easily when faced with challenges or obstacles.
  - ○ Instead of confronting challenges, chooses not to attempt or invests less than full effort.

- **Pre-Competition Anxiety:**
  - ○ Experiences heightened anxiety or stress before competitions, leading to unclear thinking about the upcoming game.
- **Dwelling on Mistakes:**
  - ○ Tendency to dwell on past mistakes, negatively impacting current performances.
  - ○ Spending more time reflecting on the past instead of focusing on the present and the future.
- **Lack of Resilience:**
  - ○ Deficiency in resilience in response to failure, perceiving it as a measure of personal worth rather than an opportunity for improvement.
  - ○ Struggle to bounce back and learn from setbacks.

- **Fear of Failure Impact:**
    - Often underperform in high-stakes situations.
    - Gameplay is dictated by fear, hindering the ability to showcase true capabilities.
- **Negative Mindset:**
    - Predisposition to anticipating unfavorable outcomes on the field or court.
    - Fixation solely on the negatives instead of focusing on positives in a given situation.

Understanding and addressing these challenges is essential for athletes aiming to enhance their mental toughness, thereby elevating overall performance.

These examples underscore the pitfalls associated with a mindset lacking mental toughness. The path toward becoming a well-rounded player is inevitably blocked when such challenges dominate one's thoughts and, consequently, their performance.

Think about this: can one realistically expect to be the best version of yourself when these challenges dominate your thoughts and, consequently, impact your performance? The question now rests with you: having recognized the characteristics of a mentally tough athlete, do you confidently identify yourself as possessing mental toughness?

Response: *Yes/No*

If not, why?

What areas are you struggling with above?

Acknowledging and addressing these challenges is the first step toward developing the mental resilience needed for optimal performance in your sport. #PERSPECTIVE.

What Mental Toughness Looks Like

Now, let's explore the traits that define a mentally tough athlete, contributing not only to success in sports but also in life.

A mentally tough athlete:

- **Maintains a Positive Attitude:**
    - Sees challenges as opportunities for growth and learning.
    - Views obstacles with optimism rather than as insurmountable barriers.
- **Demonstrates Tenacity and Perseverance:**
    - Refuses to give up until goals are achieved.

- o Considers failure as a stepping stone toward success.
- **Possesses Incredible Focus and Concentration:**
  - o Blocks out distractions, maintaining a laser focus on the task at hand.
  - o Remains undeterred by external pressures, such as the noise of the crowd or the intensity of the game.
- **Shows Remarkable Resilience:**
  - o Bounces back stronger and more determined after setbacks.
  - o Views setbacks as temporary hurdles, not roadblocks.
- **Practices Excellent Stress Management:**
  - o Acknowledges stress as part of the game and develops effective coping strategies.
  - o Remains composed and calm, even under intense pressure.
- **Is Disciplined and Committed:**
  - o Understands that consistent effort and dedication are crucial for success.
  - o Recognizes that talent alone is insufficient and tirelessly works to sharpen skills.
- **Engages in Regular Self-Reflection:**
  - o Analyzes performances and actively seeks areas for improvement.

- o Confronts weaknesses with the intention of turning them into strengths.
- **Does the "Little Things":**
    - o Recognizes the importance of seemingly insignificant details in the overall process.
    - o Goes the extra mile in practice and preparation, ensuring they outwork potential opponents.

After looking at these qualities, think about your sport and the current top performers at the professional level. Do they show these traits? Now, ask yourself: Are you confident in your mental toughness? [Yes/No].

Where do you excel in these areas?

Where do you struggle?

The Invisible Weapon

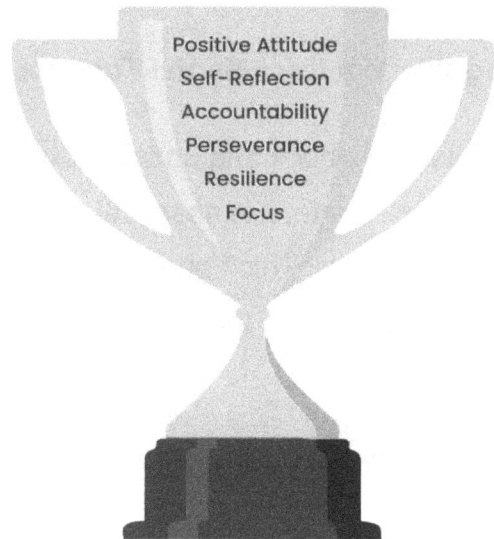

The Winning Mindset

The Losing Mindset

Gaining Wisdom from Mental Toughness Icons

As you explore this book and uncover exactly what it takes to be a mentally tough athlete, it is essential to gain inspiration and wisdom from sports legends. Think about the insightful viewpoint expressed by Billie Jean King, a tennis icon with 39 Grand Slam titles:

"Pressure is a privilege."

Analyzing this quote reveals a remarkable viewpoint. Pressure is an ever-present companion on the field or court, generating feelings of nervousness, fear, and a racing mind – normal sensations in high-pressure moments. What distinguishes Billie Jean King from many others is her perspective. She doesn't perceive pressure as a daunting challenge; instead she embraces it as an opportunity for excellence – a welcomed source of motivation to excel, prove herself, and triumph.

Consider this important idea: Winning and pressure go hand in hand. When aiming for mental toughness, adopting this mindset can make a big difference. It is not just about enduring pressure; it is about embracing it as a privilege, a clear sign that you are on the road to success.

"We focus on what we do right, we learn from what we did wrong, we move onto the next day, that's what prepares us, that's what makes us strong". - Andrew McCutchen

The Invisible Weapon

Andrew McCutchen, a 5-time All-Star and current MLB player for the Pittsburgh Pirates, delivers a powerful message that aligns with the idea of a "Growth Mindset".

This mindset involves fully committing oneself to the process and building for the future, emphasizing growth. Reflecting on successes is a powerful method to build and maintain confidence, an aspect often overlooked by athletes. Conversely, acknowledging errors or mistakes and actively learning from them ensures they won't be repeated. The key lesson is to think forward, approaching each new day with a clean slate. Focusing on the present and the future rather than dwelling on the past helps athletes succeed, showcasing the qualities of a mentally tough athlete.

"We all have different athletic strengths, but I bring a mentality, a physical toughness, an attitude, that they do not have, that helps me with the athleticism". - Arthur Jones

Arthur Jones, a decorated college football player at Syracuse University and a Super Bowl champion with the Baltimore Ravens, sheds light on how his mental toughness enhances his athleticism on the field. Jones attributes his unique "mentality" and "attitude" to his mental toughness, allowing him to stay ahead of the game and make significant contributions on the field. His mental sharpness enables him to act decisively in high-pressure situations, taking the initiative against opponents. Recognizing the limitations of relying solely on physical abilities, Jones emphasizes that his commitment to mental toughness and bringing a specific intensity to the game has been instrumental in his success. This underscores the importance of mental fortitude in attaining athletic excellence.

Conclusion

Mental toughness is a significant determinant that distinguishes good athletes from great ones. Simply possessing the physical attributes and skills essential for success is not enough; one must also possess the mental strength and attitude to fully maximize their potential as a college athlete. Those who grasp this concept, exemplified by athletes like Arthur Jones, Andrew McCutchen, and Billie Jean King, are the ones who will rise above their peers and consistently stand out on the field or the court. Mental toughness is the determining factor that makes all the difference.

Chapter Three: Athlete Resilience

My SOPHOMORE YEAR OF HIGH-SCHOOL stands out as a truly memorable period for me. I was deeply immersed in competitive junior tennis, and my progress was gaining significant momentum, reflecting in both my state and national rankings. It was a solid year filled with victories in various tournaments, catching the attention of college coaches across different levels. I could feel the momentum, filled with confidence, sensing that elusive moment when everything falls into place. However, this euphoria came to a screeching halt in the finals of a tournament in Houston.

Leading up to the finals, I had triumphed in two consecutive three-set matches, displaying resilience and skill to outwork and outplay my opponents. Confidence was at an all-time high, and I genuinely believed that no one could match my skill on the court. Winning this particular tournament would propel me into the top 20 in state rankings, bringing me closer to realizing my dream of being recruited by a top-notch college program.

I competed against my final opponent many times in previous years and never tasted defeat, never even being seriously challenged. Naturally, I felt very sure of myself heading into the finals. Little did I know that this would mark a crucial moment in my journey.

The match unfolded flawlessly, with me holding serve, breaking my opponent's serve, working points, and executing every move flawlessly. Cruising to a 4-0 lead, serving at 40-30, the anticipation of victory hung in the air. As my opponent hit a short ball, I aggressively rushed to the net. Then it happened – a distinct *SNAP* echoed just before I crashed onto the court, clutching at my ankle, which felt like it was on fire and exploding with pain.

As I looked down, I saw my ankle bulging out of my shoe, and in that moment, everything I had painstakingly worked for and all my aspirations came crashing down. Attempting to stand up and put weight on it proved futile. Forced to take an injury timeout, I watched my ankle swell to the point where my shoe could no longer contain it, ultimately leading to my decision to default the match. Believing it was a severe ankle sprain, I scheduled a doctor's appointment for the next day. However, the diagnosis delivered a crushing blow – it was a clean break.

Seated on the doctor's table, hearing that I would be out for 3-4 months, and watching them encase my leg in a cast from knee to ankle, a wave of despair overcame me. I couldn't shake the feeling that everything had gone terribly wrong, and in an instant, my dreams were unexpectedly shattered. Tuning out my parents and the doctor, my mind was consumed with relentless, repetitive thoughts: "What am I going to do now? I'll never play this well again. What am I going to do now?".

I wish that I could say breaking my ankle while in the finals was a minor setback in my blossoming junior career. I wish that I could look back on that day and see it as nothing more than a minor road bump. Unfortunately, that was not the case. The image of getting my cast in the doctor's office became a symbol of a new theme in my life – coping with failures and setbacks.

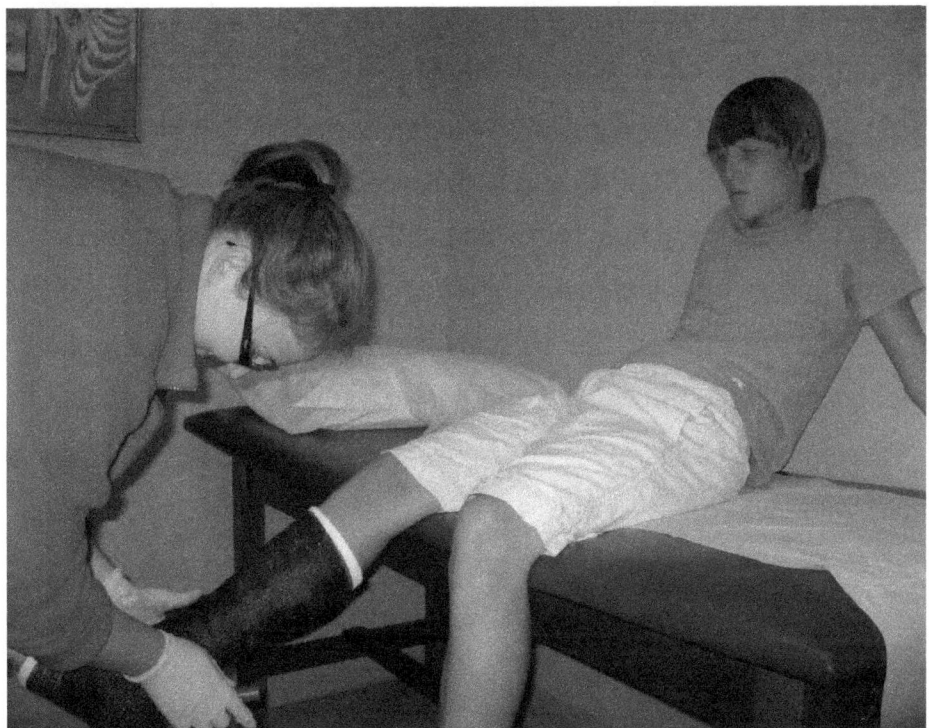

The first major setback in my tennis career (2008)

Coping with Failures & Setbacks

Failures and setbacks are part of an athlete's everyday life, appearing as losses, injuries, burnout, and various challenges such as coaches or teammates departing. These difficulties, with their varying levels of disappointment and frustration, impact an athlete's mental well-being in the short and long term, influencing their performance. Managing these challenges becomes a crucial aspect of an athlete's journey.

In reality, athletes are faced with two options when confronted with setbacks. The first option involves succumbing to despair, losing hope, giving up, postponing efforts, or engaging in the blame game by pointing fingers at parents, coaches, or teammates. It's undeniably the easier path, providing an escape route from accountability. Unfortunately, this choice is made daily by many athletes, contributing to individuals quitting their sport, losing passion, or simply remaining within their comfort zone, avoiding the steps necessary for achieving success.

On the flip side, the second choice requires that the athlete recognizes their current situation and actively seeks ways to handle and overcome challenges. This route demands dedication, involves hardships, and often feels like a tough journey. Choosing this path makes an athlete resilient and stronger when dealing with adversity. Despite being more difficult, it showcases an athlete's character and determination.

Certainly, the first option is tempting, and many individuals yield to its attraction. However, the more challenging second option is where genuine growth and strength come to the forefront. It's a demanding commitment, pushing athletes to their limits. The decision ultimately lies solely with the athlete. They are the ones who can make the choice. At some point in every athlete's career, they face this crossroads – confronted with the decision between the easy way out and the more challenging but rewarding path. It is at this moment that reality sets in, requiring athletes to define the kind of person and athlete they aspire to be.

"The hard days are the best because that's where champions are made" - Gabby Douglas

Step One: Acceptance

So, when you find yourself facing challenges in college sports – be it due to injury, a lack of playing time, a missed game-winning shot, a costly mistake or just navigating a tough period – setbacks and failures become an inevitable part of the journey. Whether you are preparing to play college or already navigating this terrain, it is crucial to acknowledge that these hurdles are part of the game. While the "pull your bootstraps up and push forward" mindset is admirable, it is equally important to recognize the impact that setbacks and failures can have on your mental state. Ignoring them might offer temporary relief, but they have a way of resurfacing at critical moments.

The first step in overcoming these challenges in your sport is acceptance. Acceptance is a powerful concept, different from giving up or resignation. It involves acknowledging the adversity, understanding it, and making a conscious choice to move forward. Resignation, on the other hand, involves being aware of the problem but giving in to the belief that nothing can be done – a pitfall that is easy to fall into.

To move toward acceptance, it is essential to grasp its true meaning and clear up common misconceptions. Acceptance does not mean being okay or content with your situation. Rather, it involves acknowledging your circumstances quickly and using them as motivation to move forward.

Contrary to another misconception, acceptance does not mean giving up on efforts to change your circumstances. It does not mean you stop trying to overcome challenges or achieve your goals. In this context, acceptance is about recognizing and understanding your current reality and the circumstances surrounding it, then coming up with a strategy to move forward despite the obstacles.

A third misconception to clear up is that acceptance equates to failure. Quite the opposite – acceptance should be seen as a powerful and resilient stance. It involves facing the truth in your situation without admitting defeat. When confronted with failures or setbacks, choosing acceptance is not a sign of weakness; instead, it signifies strength. By embracing acceptance, you assertively confront adversity, refusing to let it dictate the trajectory of your college career.

This exercise involves acknowledging and understanding the distressing situation, objectively noting the reality, and determining actionable steps to move forward.

The Invisible Weapon

1) **Distressing Situation:** Identify and write down the distressing situation you are experiencing right now.

2) **Emotion or Feeling:** Write down the emotion or feeling that you are currently experiencing in response to the situation.

3) **Thoughts or Beliefs:** Document the thoughts or beliefs you have about the situation.

4) **The Reality:** Write down the reality of the situation, as objectively as possible.

5) **What Can I Change:** Identify what you can change about the situation or what you can do to move forward.

Step Two: Changing Perspectives

THOUGHTS VERSUS REALITY

Distressing Situation:
Identify and write down the distressing situation you are experiencing right now. _____

_____
_____
_____
_____
_____

Emotion or Feeling:
Write down the emotion or feeling that you are currently experiencing in response to the situation. _____

_____
_____
_____
_____
_____

Thoughts or Beliefs:
Document the thoughts or beliefs you have about the situation. _____

_____
_____
_____
_____
_____

The Invisible Weapon

The Reaility:
Write down the reality of the situation, as objectively as possible.

_____

_____

_____

_____

_____

_____

What Can I Change:
Identify what you can change about the situation or what you can do to move forward.

_____

_____

_____

_____

_____

_____

"The moment you have a certain thought and believe it, you will experience an immediate emotional response. Your thought actually creates the emotion" - David D. Burns, M.D.

Moving beyond acceptance, the second crucial step is changing the way you think, reframing the mind. The mind can be a reliable ally or a formidable adversary, with our thoughts swinging between positive support and toxic negativity and self-criticism. Changing the way you think, involves the intentional replacement of negative or harmful thoughts with positive, empowering, and productive perspectives. This process is key to speeding recovery from setbacks, fostering resilience, and cultivating a renewed mindset.

The challenge lies in quieting the noise and breaking free from a toxic mental loop during tough times. The answer is found in a well-established technique used in counseling and sports psychology: reframing our thoughts. But what does that entail?

Reframing the mind is the art of substituting negative or harmful thoughts with more constructive ones in a given situation. Its purpose is to shift your mindset from a negative perspective to a positive, empowering, and productive one. This allows you to navigate failures and setbacks in a new way, propelling you back on track with a rejuvenated mindset. Essentially, it is a process of reprogramming your mind to think more effectively, especially in challenging situations or pressure moments during sports. In essence, you are actively building resilience!

Consider this analogy: driving on a highway where your lane is riddled with cracks, bumps, and potholes, causing your car to shake, damaging the tires and frame, and ultimately slowing you down. In this scenario, the bumpy road represents your negative thoughts, and your car symbolizes your mind. By switching lanes from the bumpy road to a smooth one, your car does not suffer, enabling it to perform better, similar to driving faster. In the same way, reframing your thoughts means shifting from a negative to a productive/positive perspective, resulting in clearer thinking, less negativity, reduced overthinking, and improved performance.

Positive Mindset **Negative Mindset**

 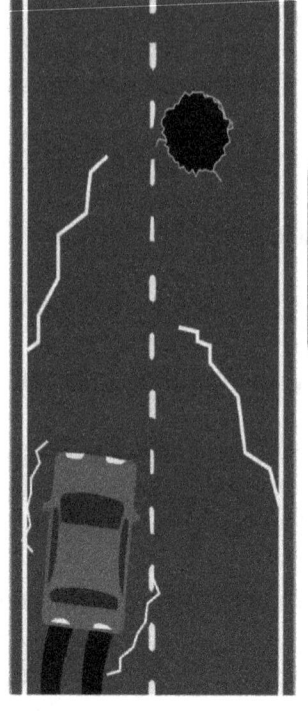

Now, let's explore the effective process of reframing your thoughts, basically changing the mental lanes you navigate. The first crucial step is to become **aware** of the thoughts running through your mind and the **language** you use when describing yourself or a situation. Often, these negative thoughts stem from our *past experiences* or *current circumstances* beyond our control. It's crucial to recognize and acknowledge them to address them in a healthy manner.

The Invisible Weapon

After becoming aware of negative thoughts, the next important step is to actively change them. This means taking a negative thought and imagining how it would sound if it was positive. For example, if your initial thought was "I can't do this," reframing it could be "I can give my best effort and learn something new along the way." This intentional change in how you see things is a powerful tool for creating a positive and empowering mindset.

Let's break down this process further and I will provide you with a worksheet that includes an example:

Step One: Identify the Negative/Harmful Thought

Explore why this thought is harmful and how it gets in the way of your progress.

Step Two: Challenge the Thought

Question and challenge the validity of the thought. Is it genuinely true?

Step Three: Reframe the Thought

Transform the negative thought into something positive or neutral.

Step One: Identify the Negative/Harmful Thought: *"I'm never going to play this good again"*

Explore why this thought is harmful and how it gets in the way of your progress: *This thought puts a "ceiling" on my future, it says that no matter what I do, it'll never be good enough.*

Step Two: Challenge the Thought

Question and challenge the validity of the thought. Is it genuinely true: *I don't think it's true or possible when I really think about it.*

Step Three: Reframe the Thought

Transform the negative thought into something positive or neutral:

"I'm never going to play this good again"
↓
"It may take a little bit of time, but when I'm healthy I will come back stronger than before."

As illustrated in my personal experience dealing with a major setback – my ankle injury – I filled out the worksheet. The dominating thought, "I'm never going to play this good again," held me captive at that moment. I believed it wholeheartedly. Looking back, I did not have anyone giving me advice and I wish I had a resource like this book to bring me back to reality. In the present tense, I filled out the sheet, delving into the weight of thought, challenging the validity, recognizing its problematic nature, and ultimately changing my perspective for the better in that situation.

How did I navigate through this without the benefit of this skill? Did things eventually work out? In simple terms, yes, they did, but it took a long time and was mentally tough for over a year. I spent a large amount of time and energy feeling negative during my recovery, always worrying about my situation and wondering if I could get back to how I was before the injury. It was really tough. I do not want you to go through something similar, or if you have already experienced it, now is your opportunity to approach it differently – use this technique. Your present and future self will undoubtedly thank you for it.

Resilient in the Face of Failures and Setbacks

By now, I hope you are growing more confident in handling failures and setbacks in your sport (which can also be useful in life). You have two important tools you can use to combat negativity: acceptance and reframing your thoughts. This final segment connects directly into reframing – changing your perspective on the challenges you are facing.

After accepting adversity and reframing your thoughts, it is time to move forward, focusing on the elephant in the room: the situation at hand. This is where the rubber meets the road and where you can genuinely start to be resilient in the face of failure and setback. View your failure or setback as a challenge to overcome – a goal to conquer. You have goals you want to set and achieve, right? The same concept applies. Encourage yourself, follow the steps outlined in the chapter, and eagerly anticipate putting in the work, both mentally and physically, to overcome the failures and setbacks you are experiencing. Do not back down; push forward.

Lastly, do not forget that resilience is a skill that can be developed over time and with practice. Each successful navigation through adversity builds your resilience. So, even when things get tough, remember that by building resilience, you will emerge on the other side stronger and more prepared for future challenges.

"All of us get knocked down, but it's resiliency that really matters. All of us do well when things are going well, but the thing that distinguishes athletes is the ability to do well in times of great stress, urgency, and pressure." - Roger Staubach

Chapter Four: Motivation

*Bleep bleep bleep**(BLARING ALARM)* disrupts the silence as Chris fumbles in the dark to silence it. After succeeding, he glances at the clock – 5:30 am on a Saturday. It marks the first day of the off-season for the freshman second-string quarterback. Sitting up in bed, Chris stretches, takes a deep breath, and declares aloud to himself (and his still-sleeping roommate), "Alright, man, let's get it. It starts today. Time to get to work."

Chris swiftly rolls out of bed, dons the team practice uniform, and prepares a quick breakfast of raw eggs in a cup and a blended fruit and vegetable smoothie. By 5:45 am, he's out the door heading to the university's football practice facility. Upon arrival, he's the first and only one there.

As he places his belongings in the locker, Chris gazes at two notecards and a picture taped to his door from the last game of the season. One card reads "take the hits, keep moving forward," another declares "I will accomplish my goals today," and the picture depicts Chris in uniform cradling a photoshopped trophy, captioned with "there is nothing I won't do to have this moment."

After this brief reflection, he glances at his "small-term goal sheet" with daily goals written on it. Chris closes the locker, ties his running shoes, and embarks on a two-hour gym workout, followed by an extra hour practicing throws with the determination of a man fiercely committed to his goals. Fired up and motivated, Chris is focused on earning the starting quarterback position in the upcoming months. No one, not even the coaches or trainers, knows that he likes being alone. Chris doesn't need external motivation; he's driven solely by his own determination.

BLEEP BLEEP BLEEP *(BLARING ALARM)* shatters the quiet as John fumbles for his phone, silences the alarm, and decides, "Not today, it's time to chill, it's officially the off-season." With a throbbing headache and sore body from celebrating the success of his junior year as the starting quarterback the night before, John falls back asleep.

As he drifts off, thoughts of the records he set and the personal and team success that was achieved this year fill John's mind. Dreaming about the victories he could secure for the team next year and the attention he might get from the media and girls makes John smile. Many hours later, he wakes to find messages from his head coach, asking about the first day of the off-season, his plans for improvement, and his goals for the upcoming season.

The Invisible Weapon

Chuckling to himself, John crawls out of bed, cracks open an energy drink, and navigates through beer cans and pizza boxes to his kitchen for a pop tart. As he munches, he dismissively thinks, "I'm the best out there; I'll kill it next year. Coach needs to chill...Chris isn't taking my spot, he's just a try-hard."

Reflecting on the past year, John considers his head coach's persistent texts and motivational pushes during practices. He recalls the coach urging him to push harder and work more, but John often performed at half-pace, occasionally spurred on by momentary motivation. Convinced of his talent as the ultimate factor in sports, John questions the need to exert more effort. In his mind, motivation is unnecessary; talent should be sufficient.

However, a poignant quote echoes: *"You can't have a million dollar dream on a minimum wage work ethic."* This serves as a stark reminder that talent alone may not be enough; a strong work ethic is essential for turning dreams into reality.

Introduction to Motivation in Sports

Motivation in sports revolves around a **profound desire to achieve**. Athletes who are highly motivated set lofty goals and tirelessly strive to attain them. This quality is marked by **perseverance and resilience**, meaning even when facing challenges, motivated athletes keep going in their training and competitions. Essentially, motivation serves as the driving force pushing individuals toward greatness in their chosen sport.

No doubt, motivation plays an essential role in an athlete's success. It stands as the deciding factor that can make a difference between victory and defeat. Without motivation, it's difficult to maintain focus and put in the extra effort that is required to excel in sports. While external sources like coaches, teammates, friends, and family can help with motivation, the ultimate source lies within oneself. Each person's level of motivation is influenced by their own personal circumstances and how much they desire to win. The reality is clear: success in sports hinges on personal motivation; it cannot be delegated to others. The results one seeks are closely connected to the depth of their own motivation and determination.

Intrinsic VS Extrinsic Motivation

While motivation is a familiar concept, it's important to explore its scientific aspects, especially the difference between intrinsic and extrinsic motivation. This is crucial for building the ideal drive that can push athletes to the next level.

Intrinsic Motivation

The first type, intrinsic motivation, is fueled by internal factors that inspire athletes. It encompasses the pure enjoyment of the sport, personal fulfillment, and the thrill of competition. Characteristics coming from within include autonomy, mastery, and purpose. Autonomy involves working independently, demonstrated by athletes who willingly put in the extra work in the gym or pursue independent activities to enhance their skills. Mastery is derived from finding satisfaction in becoming more skilled within the sport, illustrated by a tennis player mastering an effective and consistent kick serve.

Purpose involves the feeling that one's efforts matter, contributing to a larger, future-oriented goal. Athletes with high intrinsic motivation possess a genuine passion for their sport. They find joy in practicing and competing just for the sake of doing it. They play because they love it. They are driven by passion and a personal desire to be the best player they can be, not just for external rewards.

Chris, introduced at the chapter's onset, epitomizes an intrinsically motivated athlete. His burning desire to secure the starting quarterback position led him to make autonomous decisions, waking up early for an off-season workout and adorning his locker with motivational quotes. His choice to Photoshop a picture of himself with a trophy as a daily source of inspiration was entirely self-driven. Chris's actions are an embodiment of intrinsic motivation, fulfilling autonomy, mastery, and purpose simultaneously. The question posed invites a unanimous response: How confident are you that Chris will eventually fulfill his dream of becoming the starting quarterback for this team? Do you think Chris will absolutely, without a doubt, achieve his dream of being the starting quarterback for the team? Pick one: 100% or absolutely, positively, without a doubt 100%!

Extrinsic Motivation

The second type of motivation, known as "extrinsic," involves external incentives that drive athletes to excel, such as trophies, financial rewards, or social recognition. Athletes with high extrinsic motivation are propelled by the desire for real rewards, fame, and the admiration of others. While compensation and rewards are primary motivators for extrinsic motivation, an additional factor comes into play – punishment.

Athletes with high extrinsic motivation engage in their sport for the rewards and recognition that come with winning. Whether it's the money, the trophy, or media attention, extrinsically motivated athletes focus primarily on real, tangible results. Their mindset is often narrower, fixated solely on wins or losses. They may not find pleasure in the process, don't pay much attention to getting better in the future, and their motivation to put in extra work often stems from external sources like coaches, parents, or teammates. The concept of punishment becomes significant for extrinsically motivated athletes, driving them to put in extra effort, go the extra mile, or be team players out of fear of repercussions from coaches or parents.

Take John, introduced at the chapter's beginning, as an example of an extrinsically motivated athlete. John doesn't feel compelled to invest extra effort in the off-season, on the practice field, or in the gym during the season. His primary motivation comes from his coach, who pushes him in practice and administers

The Invisible Weapon

punishment for lack of effort. Despite having talent, John's narrow motivational mindset sets him up for potential failure in the long run.

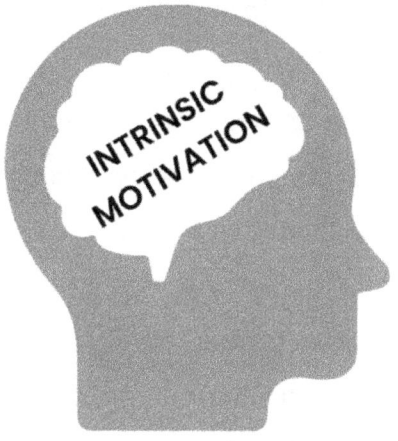 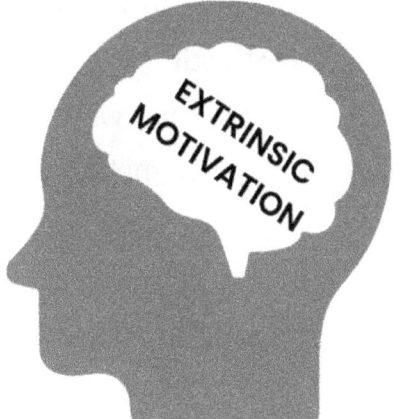

Sense of Achievement	Money
Desire to Learn	Grades
Curiosity	Praise
Interest	Career
Pride	Exams

Developing Intrinsic Motivation
Navigating Your Source of Drive

Let's take a moment to reflect on your source of motivation. Are you intrinsically or extrinsically motivated? For those naturally inclined toward intrinsic motivation, the path to success in college sports becomes clearer. If you're intrinsically motivated, fantastic! It's time to reinforce and solidify your mindset. However, if you find yourself more aligned with extrinsic motivation, there's no need to panic! The good news is that there are three ways to start shifting your mindset in the right direction, and you can implement them right away.

1. **Discovering Your Why; Unveiling the Core of Your Motivation**
    - Your "why" is the bedrock of your motivation. Whether it's making your family proud, the love of competition, or setting an example for a sibling, everyone has a driving force.
    - Focusing on your "why" provides clarity and motivation. It's natural to question your journey, but answering the classic, "Why am I doing this to myself?" becomes easier with a defined purpose.
    - Take some time during challenging times to reflect on questions like:
    - **Why did you start playing your sport?**
    - **What aspects of your sport bring you happiness?**
    - **What do you like about your sport?**
    - **Why do you continue playing your sport?**
    - **What do you want to achieve in your sport?**
    - **What qualities does your sport bring out in you?**
    - **Why are you playing in college (or want to play in college)?**

These questions provided help serve as a guide to help you through this process, giving you a real reminder of your motivation.

2. **Cultivating a Growth Mindset**

The Invisible Weapon

- A growth mindset focuses on the journey, valuing progress and personal development. In contrast, a fixed mindset fixates on outcomes, potentially hindering self-esteem and motivation.
- Embrace challenges as opportunities to grow stronger. Celebrate each step in your journey, irrespective of the pace or obstacles.
- A growth mindset builds motivation by emphasizing the process. By focusing on the small goals, building for the future, and preparing for pivotal moments, you stay motivated and hungry.

I can learn anything I want to.	I'm either good at it or I'm not.
When I'm frustrated, I persevere.	When I'm frustrated, I give up.
I want to challenge myself.	I don't like to be challenged.
When I fail, I learn.	When I fail, I'm no good.
Tell me I try hard.	Tell me I'm smart.
If you succeed, I'm inspired.	If you succeed, I feel threatened.
My effort and attitude determine everything.	My abilities determine everything.

Now, a question to ponder:

Which mindset does **Chris** have?

Which mindset does **John** have?

3. **Setting Achievable Goals**
    - Establish short and long-term achievable goals on a daily, weekly, and monthly basis (small term goals: daily and weekly, long term goals: monthly). While a detailed discussion on goal-setting awaits in later chapters, understand this: short-term goals are a powerful tool for building and maintaining motivation. If you frequently set and achieve them, you demonstrate hunger and motivation.
    - Imagine not having concrete goals to work towards. Setting achievable goals provides direction, especially on off days or when motivation wavers.
    - Consider Chris, who meticulously planned short-term goals for the day, staying motivated to accomplish them for long-term improvement. On the flip side, observe John, lacking goals and a plan, making it challenging to find motivation. Two different scenarios, likely leading to two different futures.

In summary, your journey to success in college sports hinges on your intrinsic motivation. Whether rediscovering your "why," adopting a growth mindset, or setting achievable goals, these strategies will shape your mindset and pave the way for enduring success. Remember, it's not just about the destination; it's about enjoying every step of the journey.

GOAL SHEET

Daily Goals: _____
_____
_____

Weekly Goals: _____
_____
_____

Monthly Goals: _____
_____

Maintaining Motivation on the Good Days:
Navigating Success in Sports

Ah, the good days – those times in sports when everything seems to line up, personal victories stack up, and success feels within reach. Yet, BEWARE, as this can be a tricky and risky phase. It's easy and natural to take it easy and celebrate your success, but that's where the danger lies. It is easy and completely normal to slack off, to postpone things because you are enjoying your success. However, the moment you ease up because of your achievements, you are essentially choosing to go backward. Why? Because it becomes tougher to improve and stay motivated when you are too content and satisfied with your current standing.

Celebrate your success, but don't succumb to complacency. Here are strategies to maintain and build your motivation on the good days:

Recognize Comfort and Complacency
- Be aware of signs of comfort: altered routines, skipped practices, and a relaxed mindset.
- Monitor your inner dialogue: maintain the same level of self-discipline, avoid procrastination, and resist thoughts of having done "enough."
- Bring awareness to any comfort or complacency-induced behaviors and ask yourself, "Am I getting too comfortable or complacent with my actions?"

Self-Awareness is Key
- Conduct a personal inventory: reassess your actions, commitments, and drive.
- Stay vigilant in recognizing any shift towards comfort and complacency.
- Initiate a personal reset when needed to reignite your drive and stay on the right track.

Awareness is your ally. By regularly evaluating your mindset and actions, you ensure that success doesn't breed complacency but serves as a stepping stone for sustained motivation and continuous improvement.

Reflect on Past Struggles and Current Results
- Take time to reflect on your journey, acknowledging past struggles and celebrating recent achievements.

- Recognize the progress made and use it as a source of motivation to propel yourself forward.
- Revisit the challenges you overcame, instilling the drive and focus needed for continued success.

Challenge Yourself Through Inner Dialogue (Self-Talk)
- Act as your own coach, especially when success doesn't warrant external scrutiny.
- Create motivating phrases for self-talk, like "How can I get better TODAY," "What can I do TODAY to make a DIFFERENCE," or "What I do TODAY decides the FUTURE."
- Use these phrases to stay focused and remind yourself of your goals, fostering a growth mindset and maintaining motivation.

Remember, success should not breed complacency; it should fuel a relentless pursuit of improvement. Stay aware, reflect on your journey, and challenge yourself daily through positive self-talk to ensure sustained motivation on the path to greatness.

"Complacency is the last hurdle standing between any team and its potential greatness" - Pat Riley

Motivation Through the Storm: Overcoming Bad Days

The bad days in sports can be mentally challenging, questioning your commitment and the worth of your efforts. These are the bad days, the days when motivation waivers, and the pursuit of playing in college appears burdensome. It's time to reshape that mentality, to rally against the resistance within. Here are three strategies to unearth motivation and reset those challenging days:

1. **Reconnect with Your "Why"**
- Reflect on Your Passion: In challenging times, revisit the reasons you fell in love with your sport. What brings you joy? What aspects resonate with you?
- Why Do You Do This? Ask yourself why you embark on this journey. Your "why" serves as a compass, guiding you back to your intrinsic motivations.
- Remind and Rejuvenate: Actively remind yourself of your "why" to reignite the spark and infuse positivity into your sports outlook.
2. **Champion Daily Consistency**
- Gradual Progress: On bad days, focus on incremental steps rather than lofty goals. Aim to achieve a bit more than the day before, fostering gradual progress.
- Conscious Effort: Be aware of your efforts, especially when motivation wanes. Combat inconsistency by prioritizing the tasks that contribute to your improvement.
- Checklist for Success: Create a daily checklist encompassing essential elements like practice, workouts, meals, and recovery. Check them off to build a consistent routine, a foundation for sustained motivation.

"Consistency will always beat short-term intensity" –
Unknown

3. **Embrace the Process and a Growth Mindset**
- Long-Term Perspective: Remind yourself that the work invested today shapes your future success. The bad days contribute to the foundation for your victories.
- Growth Mindset in Action: Recall the growth mindset discussed earlier. Focus on the daily process, acknowledging it as a stepping stone to long-term achievement.
- Endure for Tomorrow: Consider the impact of your efforts on future successes. The work done on bad days sets the stage for triumphant performances on the good days.

Closing Thoughts: Be Like Chris

As you conclude this chapter, think back to the tales of Chris and John. Ponder upon which player is poised for enduring success. Chris, driven by intrinsic motivation and a growth mindset. He exemplifies the path to greatness. As you continue your journey, remember, it all starts with unwavering motivation. Be like Chris.

Chapter Five: Concentration and Focus

May 16th, 2013 stands out as the second most memorable day in my tennis career, and to be frank, it's the second-best day of my life. I was deeply engaged in an intense, three-hour-plus match during the semi-finals of the NJCAA National Championships. The stakes were crazy high; the whole season, the National Championship title, everything I'd been working hard for over the last seventeen years, all hung in the balance. The match was like going into uncharted territory, carrying monumental significance. The pressure was so real, and the moment felt extremely heavy. A victory in this crucial match would secure the national championship for my team, a triumph or defeat rested solely on my shoulders. This moment turned out to be one of the defining moments not only in my tennis journey but in my whole life.

The Invisible Weapon

Every athlete aspires to be the hero in a crucial moment, to be the game-changer, lifting trophies and wearing the championship ring. This was MY moment, the culmination of years of hard work. The time had come to seize it, and I had never been more prepared to compete.

During the match, I achieved a mental state of unparalleled focus. It's difficult to describe the emotions during that time, much of it remains a blur. With over 70 people as witnesses, cheering, the scorching 90+degree heat – none of it registered. A match that spanned over three hours felt like a mere 10 minutes. I achieved complete tunnel vision; the outside world became a blur, and my entire focus was on the court, my opponent, and my coach on the sideline. The tennis ball, at times, seemed like a basketball, entirely under my control, obeying my every command. My mind worked at a rapid pace, making split-second decisions while maintaining an unusual sense of calmness. It felt like my thoughts were flowing seamlessly, and everything made perfect sense. Nothing, absolutely nothing, could break my concentration. An army could have invaded the tennis facility, and I'm fairly certain I wouldn't have noticed. While this might be an exaggeration, it vividly illustrates the mental space I occupied during that match.

In pursuit of excellence, moments like these highlight the critical role of concentration and focus. They are the key to unlocking extraordinary performances on the court or field. In the following sections we'll explore the strategies and techniques that can help you develop and harness the power of unwavering concentration in your athletic pursuits.

Making things even crazier, my opponent was in the exact same mental state as I was. He was as locked in as I was, intensifying our competition. I sensed it when we stood across from each other during the coin toss at the beginning of the match. Everything fell silent, the energy built up, and as we made eye contact, we stared at each other for what felt like an hour. At that moment, I knew it would be a battle, where neither of us would back down.

It became the perfect storm, two competitors determined not only to beat the other but to destroy them. This turned out to be one of the most brutal matches of my career and one of the most satisfying wins I had ever experienced.

Over the years, I've asked myself, and others have asked me, how did I win that match? On paper I should not have won; I was lower-ranked and "outmatched" according to their coach. Was it physical? Certainly, being in the best "tennis shape" of my life played a significant role. Was it coaching? Absolutely, with my coach having been part of and coached multiple national championship teams. Was it just a "good day"? Perhaps, but there was a big difference between that day and the "good days" I had experienced in the past. Was it my strategy? With no way to prepare against my opponent, given we hadn't played before and the lack of scouting reports, strategy was more touch-and-go throughout the match. What stands out the most to me about that match was my mentality going into it and during the game. I was intensely focused; the outside world didn't exist. My concentration and focus were perfectly centered on the match. I had successfully entered the infamous and rare mental "flow state."

My dream becoming a reality (May 2013)

Flow state

You've witnessed it on TV during big games. Chances are you've encountered it throughout your career, maybe even faced opponents experiencing it. It's the "Flow State" – a state of complete immersion in the moment, with supreme mental and bodily control.

The flow state in sports is when an athlete operates at their peak, entirely focused on the task at hand. It's marked by heightened concentration, intense focus, and unshakable composure. Some characteristics of the flow state include a sense of control, loss of self-consciousness, a distorted perception of time (either slower or faster), and finding the activity itself rewarding. This happens because of the thrill of competition, pushing the athlete to perform at extraordinary levels.

Operating in a flow state can be a game-changer when facing opponents in the heat of the battle. You've probably stumbled upon it at some point in your career. Achieving this state can sometimes happen accidentally, where you unknowingly do the right things to set your mindset before a game or match. Athletes often find themselves scratching their heads, wondering how to intentionally get into the flow again.

Fortunately, after experiencing total flow during a National Championship competition, I became **OBSESSED** with understanding how to consistently achieve that sensation on the court. My obsession drove me into sports psychology, leading to the writing of this book. I immersed myself in research, reading extensively to comprehend why and how I entered the flow state, with the ultimate goal of helping fellow athletes. After years of self-education and formal study in undergraduate and master's programs, I've refined it down to two crucial mental skills: concentration and focus.

The Invisible Weapon
Concentration and Focus

Concentration is similar to the relentless mental stamina of a marathon runner, persistently committed to a task until completion. Much like a runner, it allows the mind to endure over long stretches, avoiding weariness or distraction by the scenery.

On the other hand, **focus** is the mind's ability to channel all its energy and resources towards a singular point or goal, like a powerful beam of light illuminating a specific path amid darkness. While concentration manages energy over extended distances, focus involves disregarding distractions to direct energy and resources to a single point. Concentration maintains stamina, keeping us on course, while focus provides clarity, guiding us toward our goal.

When aiming for success or seeking the flow state, a combination of focus and concentration is crucial. This creates the perfect balance, the ideal storm, especially when competing on the field or court.

Building & Maintaining Concentration

Building concentration is not just important; it is crucial for unlocking the flow state, but also for positioning yourself for victory in general. While enhancing concentration before a game is vital, maintaining it throughout the game is the ultimate goal.

Three effective methods for building and sustaining concentration are breathing exercises, visual reminders, and pre-practice/pre-performance routines.

The first approach involves practicing breathing exercises. Now, I know what you are probably thinking: "Coach George, how can something as basic as breathing, which I do every second, enhance my concentration in sports?" It's a valid question. But here's the catch: I guarantee you haven't been breathing the correct way – the intentional way.

So, what does intentional deep breathing do for athletic performance? First and foremost, it tackles the trio of anxiety, stress and pressure – the unwelcome companions in the competitive arena. Let's face it; these feelings are a natural byproduct of competition, something we grapple with before and during our play quite frequently. Controlling these emotions is the key for maintaining concentration on your game.

Consider this: anxiety, stress and pressure contribute to losing focus. Your mind might wander to the wrong things before or during a game – dwelling on the outcome, sizing up your opponent, worrying about what your coach or parents might think, or feeling the weight of the moment you're about to step into. Not ideal, right?

Enter deep breathing – a game-changer. It triggers a natural relaxation response, boosting your respiratory sinus arrhythmia (RSA), which, in turn helps diminish stress and anxiety in the moment. It also activates your parasympathetic nervous system, counteracting your body's "fight or flight" response. The result? Calmness prevails, and stress, pressure and anxiety take a back seat. Through deep breathing, you are naturally supplying your body and mind with the much-needed oxygen and nutrients. Now, that's a breath of fresh air – literally!

Let's explore the practice of deep breathing, not just as a routine but as a powerful tool to boost your performance, both before and during play.

Pre-Game Deep Breathing:

Before you step onto the court or the field, pause for a moment. Find a quiet spot without distractions. Whether standing, sitting, or lying down, place a hand on your stomach just below the ribcage. Focus on your breath, allowing your diaphragm to expand and contract. Follow this pattern for 5 minutes:
1. Deep breath in through your nose (lasts 5-10 seconds)
2. Deep breath out through your mouth (lasts 5-10 seconds)

Repeat.

As you breathe, shift your thoughts to the upcoming game – your strategy, game plan, and the actions you need to take. This practice calms your body and clears your mind, setting the stage for focused and optimal performance. Consistency is key; make this a pre-game ritual to maximize its impact.

In-Game Deep Breathing:

During play, especially in high-pressure moments, your body and mind might scream for attention. You may feel as if you are in crisis mode because things may not be going your way and you hit a wall. If you find yourself losing concentration, deploy the "object technique" for a quick reset. Here's how:

1. Identify a circular or square object nearby.
2. Focus on a starting point (corner for square, any point for a circle).
3. Inhale deeply though your nose, tracing the object's perimeter with your eyes.
4. Exhale through your mouth, continuing to follow the object's border.

Repeat.

Engaging in this brief breathing exercise serves as a mental reset. By shifting your focus to deep breaths and tracing the chosen object's perimeter, you bring your attention back to the present moment. This intentional redirection provides your mind with a break from the overwhelming physical and mental distractions, allowing it to recalibrate. Consider it as a quick snap back to attention, a valuable tool to regain focus and realign your mental state during critical moments of play.

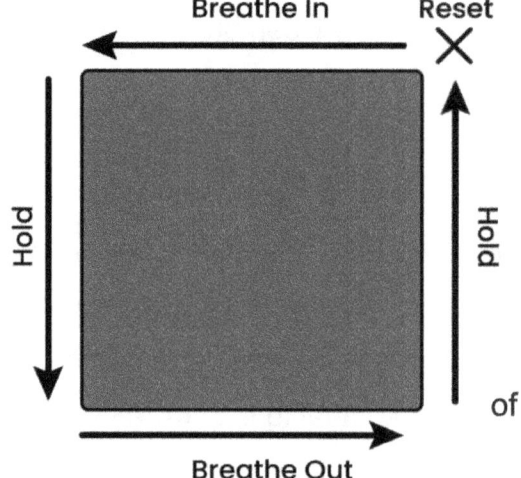

The Invisible Weapon

Visual Reminders for Concentration

The second technique to build and sustain concentration involves using visual reminders. These cues possess the ability to trigger powerful emotional responses, redirecting your focus towards the essential elements for victory. In moments of distraction during practice or a game, visual reminders can guide your concentration back to what's important. Your visual cues can range from a simple notecard, a piece of tape, to a colored wristband. Experiment to find what grabs your attention and is easily identifiable. Personally, I preferred a yellow or green notecard placed on my tennis bench, visible from anywhere on the court. Once you have identified an effective visual reminder, add phrases, words, or even pictures that will trigger a strong mental response. Whenever you glance at your visual reminder, concentrate on its content, allowing you to "snap back to reality." For instance, my notecards either contained elements of my pre-devised game plan or encouraging phrases. Whenever I sensed a lapse in concentration during a match, a glance at my notecard, a deep breath, and I was back in the zone.

One of the notecards I used in my playing days to regain concentration (2010's)

Establishing Pre-Performance Routines

The third method to boost concentration involves having a set pre-practice/pre-performance routine. This means engaging in the same activities before every match or performance to foster a calm, composed mental state. Your routine could include stretching, muscle rolling, dynamic exercises, donning a specific piece of clothing, listening to music, or practicing deep breathing techniques. This routine creates consistency and familiarity in an otherwise uncomfortable situation. By engaging in familiar activities, you relax both your mind and body, finding comfort in the midst of discomfort. Pre-match routines aim to help you feel at ease, providing a sense of control and comfort, allowing you to concentrate fully on the upcoming game. Establishing and consistently practicing these routines are crucial to entering a concentrated state before each game or match.

> **Pre-Match Routines**
>
> 1) Spend 5 minutes deep breathing
> 2) Dynamic warm-up / band exercises
> 3) 30-minute warm-up on tennis court
> 4) 5 minutes deep breathing w/ a focus on upcoming match
> 5) Listen to pre-match music as I walk to the court
>
> **FIGHT!   EXECUTE!**

My pre-match routine notecard from playing in college (2015)

The Invisible Weapon
Building and Maintaining Focus

We all have the ability to focus or concentrate, a skill we regularly use when we move our attention from one thing to another. Constant focus is essential; without it, tasks would remain undone. In the world of sports, developing this skill is an immediate advantage. However, the challenge for me and many athletes wasn't a lack of focus but directing it toward the right things.

During my college playing days, my focus was sharp, but not always on the right things. There were instances where I fixated more on spectators or the happenings around me than on the game. I vividly recall a match played outdoors where the aroma of grilling steaks wafted from nearby, and I found myself strategizing on how to get a steak for dinner rather than on winning the match. It's a common occurrence, we are always focusing, but not necessarily on the crucial aspects: our opponents' movements, game strategy, shifts in dynamics, our energy levels, and execution.

Staying focused is crucial in our mental game, and the following strategies can help with that: focusing on the things you can control, using cue words, and asking yourself questions to stay focused.

Focusing on the Controllables

First and foremost, athletes naturally like to be in control, attempting to manage everything, from diet, how they sleep, game preparation, their uniforms, and even the results of the game. However, the unpredictable nature of sports often challenges this control. It's a bit like playing cards at a casino; despite thinking we have control, the truth is, things don't always go the way we expect. Our focus tends to gravitate toward elements we believe we can control – our preparation, strategy, gameplay, and even the outcome. Engaging in an exercise to identify these controllables can be enlightening. (I highly encourage you to complete the exercise before you continue).

Circle of Control Exercise

INSTRUCTIONS:

Place items from the word bank **INSIDE** the circle if you believe you can control them.

Place items from the word bank **OUTSIDE** the circle if you cannot control them.

The Invisible Weapon
Inside = Control | Outside = Can't Control

Word bank:

outcome, personal performance, teammates, warm-up(s), attitude, communication, opposing player comments, opposing crowd, percentages, results, referees/umpires, schedule of events, weather, media, facilities, altitude, teammates run correct play, opponent is faster, ball is too flat/too bouncy, concentration, teammates don't pass the ball, strategy, opponents' strategy, effort, coach's opinion, teamwork, technique, sleep, nutrition

Debrief

1) After you finish, look back at your circle, ask yourself if these are things that you have **100%** control over.
2) Feel free to add/remove any elements you have written down that are or aren't under our **100%** control.
3) The only things that should belong and remain in the middle of the circle are three words: Attitude, Concentration, and Effort. These are the only three things that you have complete, 100% control over.

By looking at sport in this way will put things into a new and fresh perspective right? In all reality, we have little control in our sport besides the big three: Attitude, Concentration, and Effort.

Cue Words

Using "cue words" is another way to maintain focus during practice or play. These words act as reminders of your goals, what you need to focus on, and your intentions. They are like alarms in your head that go off when you say or think the cue word. Examples could include powerful words like "Compete," "Confidence," "Execute," or even a simple yet impactful word like "Focus." Here are the factors contributing to the formation of effective cue words:

- **Simplicity:**

The Invisible Weapon

- Cue words are brief and straightforward, allowing athletes to swiftly refocus their attention on the task at hand.
- **Specificity:**
  - Each cue word is customized to address an athlete's unique psychological and physical needs.
- **Motivation:**
  - Cue words serve as a source of inspiration, propelling athletes beyond perceived limitation to achieve their objectives.
- **Reminders:**
  - Cue words can also serve as reminders, reinforcing technical skills or strategic aspects crucial for an athlete's performance.
- **Relaxation:**
  - Specific cue words may trigger relaxation in high-pressure situations, assisting in regulating arousal levels and reducing anxiety.

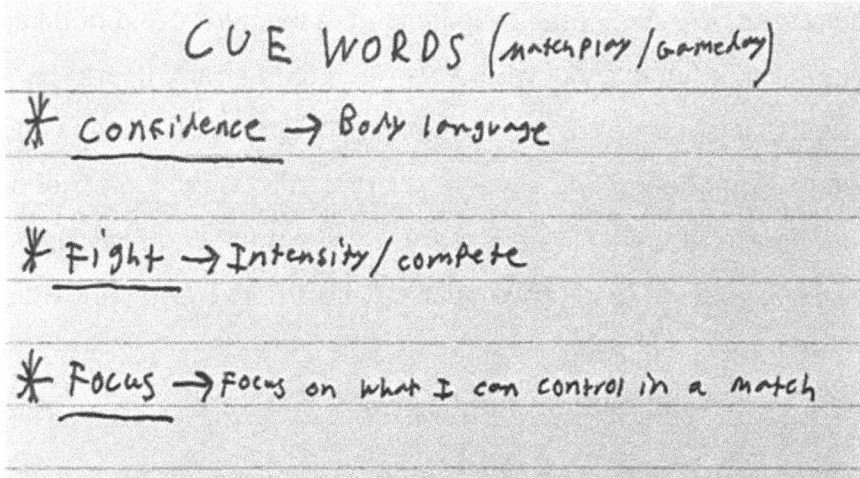

Example of cue words that I found worked for me when I played in college (2015)

The concept behind cue words is simple but powerful. When facing pressure or distraction, verbalize or think about your cue words to recenter your attention and focus on the present moment. Establishing this habit can be challenging, but here is a simple trick: the "rubber band trick." Get an ordinary rubber band or bracelet, write your cue word on it – I personally had "this moment" written on mine. When you feel the need to reset or maintain focus, snap the band on your wrist, look down, say your cue word out loud, or repeat in your mind. The snap shifts your attention, helping you regain focus, and repeating the cue word directs your attention to the right place.

Self-Questioning

Improving your focus can also be done through self-questioning. Before we get into that, it's important to realize something. Generally, athletes are not great at asking themselves questions. We don't really like looking in the mirror and admitting our flaws or figuring out where we need to improve. In sports, questioning yourself is the key to unlocking the full potential of your focus. You need to know where your mind is, what it's focused on, and how to redirect it if necessary. Here are a few questions you can ask yourself to improve your self-awareness and concentration:

- **Where is my mind right now?**

- Identify whether your thoughts are in the present moment, focused on the task at hand, or if they are wandering elsewhere.
- **What is distracting me?**
  - Pinpoint external or internal distractions that might be pulling your attention away from the game or match.
- **Am I focusing on the controllables?**
  - Reflect on whether your attention is directed towards factors within your control – attitude, concentration, and effort (A.C.E.).
- **What is my cue word right now?**
  - Recall and reaffirm your chosen cue word to realign your focus and intentions.
- **How can I bring my focus back?**
  - Develop strategies or techniques to redirect your focus when you catch it drifting away.

By incorporating self-questioning into your routine, you are not just playing the physical game; you are mastering the mental one as well. It is about being proactive in understanding your mental state, addressing distractions, and refocusing your mind on what truly matters.

Focus Questions

An additional skill for building and maintaining focus involves asking yourself "focus questions." These questions are straightforward and direct, guiding your mind to the present moment and what you need to concentrate on for success. Use them during practice or competition, preferably during a timeout or break when you have a moment to breathe. The three questions are:

1) What is my opponent or opponents doing well?
2) What is my opponent or opponents struggling with?
3) What do I need to do moving forward?

Focusing on your opponent's strengths and weaknesses provides valuable information for adjusting your game or strategy. Contemplating what you need to execute moving forward narrows your focus. Practice these questions during scrimmages until you become comfortable answering them strategically. Once you have mastered them in practice, integrate them into your next game or match, bringing crucial focus to yourself and your opponent to find winning solutions!

Concentration + Focus = Flow

At the onset of this chapter, I recounted one of my most memorable matches, an extraordinary experience where I found myself completely immersed in the flow state. My concentration and focus were precisely tuned in to the right elements, blocking out unnecessary thoughts and allowing me to operate within the flow. Since that match, and throughout my career transitioning into professional life, I sought ways to consistently unlock the flow state. Strengthening concentration through breathing exercises, visual reminders, and routines, while bolstering focus by honing in on controllables, using cue words, and employing Focus Questions, create the ideal mental storm.

Moving forward, I implore you to start using these techniques immediately. Start cultivating your concentration and focus to assess the flow state consistently. The more you integrate and practice these techniques, the more mentally prepared you will become for the challenges of your college career.

Chapter Six: Sport Confidence

Mike Tyson - The Mental Warrior

"*F*IVE MINUTES BEFORE I COME OUT while I'm in the dressing room, I'm breaking my gloves down. I'm pushing the leather to the back of my gloves, so my knuckle could pierce through. When I come out I have supreme confidence. I'm scared to death. I'm afraid. I'm afraid of everything. I'm afraid of losing. I'm afraid of being humiliated. But I'm confident. The closer I get to the ring the more confident I get. The closer, the more confident. The closer the more confident I get. All during training I've been afraid of this man. I think this man might be capable of beating me. I've dreamed of him beating me. For that I've always stayed afraid of him. The closer I get to the ring the more confident I get. Once I'm in the ring I'm a God. No one could beat me. I walk around the ring but I never take my eyes off my opponent. Even if he's ready and pumping and can't wait to get his hands on me. I keep my eyes on him. I keep my eyes on him. Then once I see a chink in his armor, boom, one of his eyes may move, and then I

The Invisible Weapon

know I have him. Then once he comes to the center of the ring he looks at me with his piercing look as if he's not afraid. But he already made that mistake when he looked down for that one tenth of a second. I know I have him. He'll fight hard for the first two or three rounds, but I know I broke his spirit. During the fight I'm supremely confident. I'm making him miss and I'm countering. I'm hitting him to the body; I'm punching him real hard. And I'm punching him, and I'm punching him, and I know he's gonna take my punches. He goes down, he's out. I'm victorious. Mike Tyson, greatest fighter that ever lived" - **Mike Tyson**

Mike Tyson, a legendary figure in sports history, goes beyond mere victory; he aimed not only to win but to dominate with an unmatched savagery unparalleled in the world of boxing. His physical abilities made him a freak of nature, but it was his strong mental strength that elevated him to the status of a true powerhouse in the sport.

Tyson's journey from the streets of Brooklyn to becoming a boxing legend is a story worth exploring. Raised by a single mom, in very challenging circumstances, he resorted to breaking and entering for financial survival. Interestingly, Tyson, with a speech impediment and wasn't the biggest kid on the block, dealt with severe bullying. However, what he lacked in physical size, he made up for with a relentless, unstoppable mental strength. Even in the street fights against older and stronger opponents, Tyson showed a natural ability to switch into a determined, fiery mindset, emerging as an unstoppable force.

A turning point came when Tyson, serving time in juvenile detention, crossed paths with the legendary boxing coach Cus D'Amato. D'Amato, recognizing Tyson's potential, took him under his wing in Catskill, New York. D'Amato's coaching style, highlighting mental development alongside physical training, proved unconventional yet highly effective. From the outset, D'Amato subjected Tyson to relentless mental challenges – building him up only to break him down repeatedly.

D'Amato did not just teach Tyson to work hard but also gave him unmatched confidence. Knowing that confidence was the key missing ingredient in Tyson's impressive skill set, D'Amato worked extremely hard to build it up. He taught Tyson how to control his emotions, maintain focus, and rise above everyday distractions. D'Amato's influence was transformative, turning Tyson into one of the most self-assured and powerful athletes on the planet.

Tyson's boxing record is impressive, with 50 wins and 44 by knockout, proving that confidence played a crucial role in his success. Coach D'Amato's strong belief and mental conditioning became the driving force behind Tyson's meteoric rise.

Boxing record	
Total fights	58
Wins	50
Wins by KO	44

Losses	6
No contests	2

Confidence, as shown by Tyson, emerges as a powerful force in sports. It is not just a desirable quality but one of the most important factors – one that can be challenging to develop and easy to lose if you don't have the right mindset and take the right actions.

As you go deeper into this chapter, take a moment to assess your own confidence with the Confidence Inventory Test. This sets the stage for your journey towards unbreakable self-assurance.

CONFIDENCE QUESTIONAIRRE

Answer all questions on a scale of 1-10, with 10 being the best and 1 being the worst.

How confident are you in your ability to
perform under pressure during a game? _____

How confident are you in maintaining
a high level of performance, even
when things are not going as planned? _____

How confident are you in your ability
to execute your sporting skills successfully? _____

How confident are you in your ability to
bounce back after a mistake during a game? _____

How confident are you in your ability to perform
your best when you are under physical strain? _____

How confident are you in your ability to
mentally stay focused during a game? _____

How confident are you that you can
handle the pressure from spectators
or media during a match? _____

How confident are you in your ability to maintain
your performance level despite distractions? _____

How confident are you in your ability to
execute your game plan, even when
faced with strong opposition? _____

How confident are you in your ability to stay
motivated throughout the entire game/season? _____

The Invisible Weapon
Understanding Confidence

In the sports world, confidence means believing strongly in your abilities. It is an unshakeable belief that pushes you onto the field, court, or track with the assurance that you can overcome any challenge. It's the confident voice in your head saying that you possess the skills, strength, and spirit to outperform yourself and beat your opponents, even when faced with daunting odds. Confidence extends beyond winning; it involves facing defeat, learning from it, and coming back stronger. It's like a well-trained athlete, who's ready to take on any opponent because of hard training, practice, and knowing their strengths and weaknesses. In sports, confidence is the calm understanding that you are ready and capable.

Imagine the feeling as you get ready for a match. You feel great, strong, and powerful. It doesn't matter who the opponent is; you are there to play and win. This self-belief makes you proud and capable – a real display of confidence. On the other hand, there's that pregame feeling of doubting yourself, where you feel poorly about your abilities, questioning if you can perform well. The worry about making mistakes or not playing well looms large, causing you to feel scared and lacking in self-belief. Confidence, a wonderful yet tricky concept, goes up and down all the time, needing balance to avoid going to extremes.

Why Athletes Gain Confidence

Understanding why athletes become more confident is crucial for learning how to build it. Athletes gain confidence by reaching their own personal goals, feeling a sense of achievement and fueling that confidence fire. Consistent training and practice contribute significantly. Regular engagement in drills and scrimmages develops these skills, builds against weaknesses, and instills confidence through repetition. Overcoming challenges or setbacks boosts confidence by showcasing personal growth and resilience.

Confidence, as we've seen, can come from many different things, not just from winning or losing. Paying attention to these things is crucial, especially in college sports, where only focusing on winning or losing can weaken overall confidence.

Why Athletes Lose Confidence

Understanding why athletes lose confidence is just as important, and the following reasons might make sense to many. The most significant factor is failure. Failing during a game or on the court can make you doubt your abilities, making you feel unsure. Failure to reach your goals can be discouraging, and make you question your value.

Negative influences, such as surrounding yourself with people who discourage or criticize without giving constructive feedback, can also wear away at your confidence. Negativity can spread, especially on a college team with below average results. Additionally, factors off the field or court, like personal, social, or academic life, can affect confidence. This shows how everything in an athlete's life is connected.

Ultimately, when an athlete loses confidence, it often goes back to a failure or the perception of a failure, highlighting how setbacks can really mess with your mind.

Building Confidence

Building confidence in sports can be challenging, especially when it's all about whether you win or lose. The stark reality in sports is that you often have more losses than wins, a fact particularly true in individual sports. Many college athletes struggle with confidence because they are concentrating on the wrong things – like whether they win or lose – instead of the steps they take to get there. As you go through this chapter, pay attention and keep in mind that the confidence-building skills mentioned don't depend on winning or losing. This is extremely crucial for improving your mental game.

Self-Talk Confidence Builder

A helpful way to build confidence is through self-talk, a powerful force that is always at work in our minds, influencing our thoughts, feelings, and emotions in different situations. In the world of sports, talking to yourself in a positive, encouraging, and confident way can be a game-changer, guiding you toward success in moments of intense competition.

Self-talk comes in three impactful forms for building confidence: mantras, reminders, and statements.

Mantras are short words or phrases that you repeat to boost your confidence during pressure-filled situations. Examples include saying things like "You can do this," "execute," "why not me, why not us," "you are built for this," and "this moment is mine." For everyday confidence outside of competition, you might use mantras like "I am worthy." "I am capable," "I am doing enough," and "I am growing every day." These short, focused phrases should really connect with you, so experiment during practice to find what helps you mentally.

Reminders act like signals in your self-talk, reminding you of your capability to overcome challenges, affirming that you belong in that moment and you can come out on top. Examples include "I've been here before," "I've executed this shot/play before," "this is nothing compared to what I've been through," "I am capable," "I've worked for this moment," and "I've worked for this chance," Repeating these reminders when doubt surfaces or when confidence is shaky can significantly impact how you think and perform.

Statements are powerful affirmations that reinforce your goals, intentions, and abilities. Examples include saying things like "I am a great competitor," "I will succeed in this competition," "I am strong and capable," and "My hard work will pay off." This kind of self-talk is a powerful tool to boost confidence when you need it the most.

As you try out these self-talk strategies, remember that building confidence is about more than just outcomes; it is about the inner processes that elevate your mental game.

Step-By-Step Guide to Creating a "Confident Self-Talk Dialogue" for Athletes

1. **Identify Negative Thoughts:** Begin by acknowledging any negative or self-defeating thoughts that surface. Pay attention to internal dialogues that create doubt, weaken confidence, or make you anxious about your performance.
2. **Question Negative Thoughts:** Once identified, challenge these thoughts. Question if they are true and determine whether they are rooted in reality or just assumptions and fears. Realizing that these thoughts might not have much substance can make them less powerful and can weaken their impact.
3. **Replace Negative Thoughts With Positive Ones:** Take proactive steps to replace negative thoughts with positive and encouraging statements. For every negative thought, create a corresponding positive one. For instance, swap "I can't do this" with "I'm capable, and I've undergone rigorous training for this moment."
4. **Create Your Confidence Mantras, Reminders, and Statements:** Develop your own motivational dialogue that

serves to boost your confidence. Come up with statements that lift your confidence and remind you of your strengths and abilities. For example, "I am resilient, I am well-prepared, and I am unstoppable."

5. **Practice Your Dialogue:** Regularly rehearse your positive self-talk dialogue. Similar to physical training, repeating these affirmations is essential for them to become a natural and automatic part of your mindset.
6. **Apply Your Dialogue:** Put your positive self-talk into action, whether you are practicing or competing. When doubts arise, rely on your dialogue to maintain your confidence and concentration.

By taking these steps, you are not only dealing with the negative thoughts; you are also building a mindset of toughness and self-confidence. Embrace this mental training as an integral part of your overall preparation for peak athletic performance.

Body Language Confidence Builder

In the world of sports, an athlete's body language serves as an unspoken language, giving us important insights into their mental state and potential performance. The way an athlete carries themselves speaks volumes – it can show confidence or uncertainty, readiness or hesitation. Picture two athletes: one looking confident with strong posture, the other seeming lost with poor posture. Even if you don't know what is going on in their minds, you would probably prefer to compete against the second athlete. This highlights how body language can impact confidence.

The connection between our minds and bodies is clear. Our minds control our bodies, and this close relationship reflects in our body language. When we feel confident, it comes through in how we stand and act. Conversely, moments of self-doubt are glaringly apparent. Coaches, players, and even fans notice these signals, just as you would when sizing up your opponents. The goal is to consistently show confidence, creating a powerful image even when you might not feel totally confident inside. This not only influences how others see you but also triggers a positive feedback loop within yourself.

Examples of confident body language:
- Maintaining eye contact
- Head level with chin up
- Shoulders pushed back, chest out
- Wide stance
- Standing up straight
- Strong, confident posture

Examples of Body language that shows a lack of confidence:
- Minimal eye contact
- Head down or to the side
- Slumped shoulders, chest not out
- Closed-off stance
- Poor posture, like sinking under pressure

Whether you are already showing confident body language or seeking improvement, the "Room-Door Technique" offers a subtle way to enhance your presence. Each time you leave a room, take a deep breath, stand up straight, and tell yourself, "I am confident," before entering the next room. Turn it into a habit, and soon, this routine will naturally help you carry yourself confidently into many different situations.

Superman Pose Technique

Here is another way to improve your confident body language: try the Superman pose in front of a mirror every day. Even if it feels a bit awkward at first, this pose has numerous benefits. Seeing yourself in a powerful stance helps your mind believe in your strength and confidence. Additionally, spending a few minutes in this pose each day increases testosterone levels and lowers cortisol, the stress hormone. This all contributes to more confidence for you.

Identifying Strengths to Boost Confidence

Finally, boosting your confidence involves recognizing your strengths. These are the special qualities and skills that define you as an athlete. Strengths can be physical or mental – things you are really good at or do exceptionally well. It could be anything from physical attributes like being flexible or having excellent cardio to mental strengths like being confident or determined. Take a moment to write down your strengths and understand why they are effective in your sport. This list can serve as a confidence booster before crucial moments in your athletic journey. Bringing focus to what you bring to the table and what you can execute effectively can provide great insight before stepping on the field or the court or even during a game or a match to remind yourself what you are capable of and how to best use what you have in the heat of competition.

As you move on to the next chapter, keep in mind that boosting your confidence is a comprehensive effort. It includes body language, how you train your mind, and understanding what your strengths are. Confidence isn't just a quality you have; it's like a language spoken through everything you do.

Part 1: Physical Strengths

Please list down your top physical strengths related to your sport. These could be endurance, speed, agility, strength, flexibility, or any other specific skill. Afterwards, identify why they are strengths and how they can be used effectively in competition.

1. _____
2. _____
3. _____

Part 2: Mental Strengths

Please list down your top mental strengths that help you in your sport. These could be focus, determination, resilience, calmness under pressure, strategic thinking, or any other mental attribute. Afterwards, identify why they are strengths and how they can be used effectively in competition.

1. _____
2. _____
3. _____

Taking the time to reflect on your strengths:

Conclusion of Chapter: Unleashing Your Inner Champion

As we conclude this chapter on boosting confidence, let us take another look at the inspiring story of Mike Tyson – a truly confident athlete. Close your eyes and envision Tyson's thoughts as he gets ready for the ring, picture how he carries himself, and imagine feeling the impact of his punches that are echoing through the arena. It's pretty intense, right? Stepping into the ring and going up against Iron Mike would be a huge challenge.

What sets Tyson apart is how he masters the elements: self-talk, body language, and a profound understanding of his strengths.

The Invisible Weapon

These are the foundations of his confidence, pushing him to incredible success. The lesson here is clear – use this mix for yourself, make it a part of who you are, and watch your confidence grow.

In the big picture of athletic achievement, Mike Tyson shows us just how vital confidence is. Learn from his example, look closely at the details in this chapter and recognize that building your confidence is a key ingredient for success in college sports.

As you move forward on this journey, remember: your self-talk is a powerful ally, your body language speaks volumes, and understanding your strengths is your secret weapon. You have the capacity to tap into your inner champion, just like Iron Mike did. So, go ahead, take in the wisdom within these pages, and start on the path to becoming the confident athlete you are meant to be. The arena awaits – make it yours.

Chapter Seven: Accountability

"My dad taught me life lessons in everything I did, he was my coach every day. Whether it was football or working at the service station, how I cut the grass, cleaned the mower. I mean there was a standard for everything we did, if you didn't meet the standard you had to do it over. There was a reckoning every day about how you did what you were supposed to do and I think that created a tremendous amount of accountability for me in terms of how I grew up. But it also taught me the importance of a partnership in terms of working with people who had a high standard for what you did and how you did it and why it was important to do it that way" - Nick Saban

The Invisible Weapon

Nick Saban is considered one of the premier college coaches in sports. He has won numerous national championships and coached several all-American players. His coaching philosophy, summed up in the phrase "**The Process**," reflects his high standards and the expectation for excellence on the field.

Coach Saban has created an environment where there is no room for average or being too comfortable. He demands peak performance from every player, promoting an environment where accountability is highly valued. Each day becomes a test for learning and improvement; every practice, game and film session serves as an opportunity for players to improve their skills. For Saban, it is not just about doing things correctly; understanding the reasons behind success or failure is equally important.

Coach Saban's commitment to excellence extends beyond the playing field, shaping individuals as much as athletes. He encourages a sense of ownership and stresses the importance of hard work and dedication. Saban believes that success is not just a wish but a result of unwavering commitment in both sports and life. While accolades and victories are significant, Saban places greater importance on the overall development of his players, making them better individuals both on and off the field.

In Coach Saban's philosophy, accountability stands out as the central principle, deeply rooted in his upbringing and visible in all aspects of his life. He acknowledges the immense power of accountability, whether applied to everyday tasks like mowing the lawn or leading championship-level football teams. Interestingly, football, a focal point in his professional life, is intentionally downplayed in his discussions on accountability. This deliberate choice underscores Saban's belief that accountability goes beyond the athletic realm, influencing every aspect of our lives.

As you explore Coach Saban's perspective, take note of the singular mention of football. This intentional exclusion highlights the strong connection between our collegiate sports experiences and our broader college life. Saban's conviction that accountability begins beyond the sports arena emphasizes a fundamental truth; our actions off the field profoundly impact our performance on it. This intricate relationship between accountability, sports, and personal life forms a vital narrative that we will explore further in this chapter.

Exploring Accountability in College Sports

Now, let's dive into how accountability specifically relates to college sports. In your athletic journey, accountability is the foundation for success. It involves taking responsibility not only for your own performance but also how your actions impact the overall success of the team. On the court, accountability wasn't just a factor – it was key to clinching a national championship and earning All-American honors in my college career. However, off court accountability became the driving force behind my journey, inspiring me to share my experiences in this book. My deep belief in the transformative power of accountability fuels my passion and highlights its crucial significance.

The Invisible Weapon

In college sports, your teammates, coaches, and even fans depend on you to fulfill your role and responsibilities. Imagine being part of a basketball team: your accountability involves attending practices and games punctually, giving your best effort, and supporting your teammates. It's about understanding that each player's commitment and effort directly influences the team's performance.

Simply put, accountability in college sports is a shared commitment to a common goal. It means realizing that your actions, both on and off the field or court, affect not only you but the entire team. This level of accountability nurtures unity and trust among teammates, creating an environment where everyone is working together.

The challenge in college sports isn't just excelling as an individual player but also contributing to the team's collective success. Accountability involves pushing yourself to achieve personal goals while acknowledging that these achievements contribute to the team's success. It requires a delicate balance of self-discipline and collaboration within the team.

Let's break down how accountability plays a role in college sports:

1. **Attendance and Punctuality:** Being accountable in college sports starts with showing up. Whether it's a practice session, a team meeting, or a game, your commitment to being present and on time is a fundamental aspect of accountability.

2. **Effort and Performance:** Your teammates rely on you to give your best effort during every practice and game. Accountability means consistently bringing your A-game and pushing yourself to improve.
3. **Supporting Teammates:** Accountability extends beyond individual performance. It involves supporting your teammates, both in successes and challenges. Being a reliable teammate fosters trust and camaraderie.
4. **Adherence to Team Rules:** Every team has its set of rules and guidelines. Being accountable means following these rules, whether they pertain to conduct, training regimes, or any other team-specific policies.
5. **Off-Field/Off Court Conduct:** Your behavior off the field or court matters. Being accountable involves making choices that reflect positively on yourself and the team. This includes managing your academics, personal life, and overall well-being.

Now, take a moment to reflect on these aspects of accountability in college sports. How are you currently measuring up? Are there areas where you can enhance your accountability to contribute more effectively to your team's success? Remember, accountability is not just a concept – it is a daily practice that shapes your journey as a college athlete.

The Invisible Weapon
The Power of Accountability

Let's explore why accountability holds such immense power, not just in the realm of sports but in shaping your character and influencing your trajectory in college and beyond.

1. **Ownership of Actions:** Accountability empowers you to take ownership of your actions. When you acknowledge your responsibilities and commit to fulfilling them, you are actively shaping your narrative.
2. **Building Trust:** In a team setting, trust is paramount. Accountability is the glue that builds and maintains trust among teammates. When each player can rely on the others to fulfill their roles, a strong foundation is established.
3. **Resilience and Growth:** Embracing accountability means embracing challenges as opportunities for growth. Instead of shying away from difficulties, accountable individuals see them as opportunities to develop resilience and enhance their skills.
4. **Cohesive Team Dynamics:** A team that operates with accountability is a well-oiled machine. Each part understands its role, works together with others, and contributes to the team's overall success. This creates a positive and motivating environment.
5. **Setting Standards:** Accountability sets the standard for excellence. When every team member is accountable, a culture of high standards is established. This culture becomes a driving force for continuous improvement.

6. **Influence on Performance:** Accountability directly influences performance. Athletes who hold themselves accountable are more likely to consistently perform at their best, contributing to individual and team success.
7. **Preparation for Life Beyond Sports:** The lessons learned through accountability in college sports extend far beyond the playing field. They prepare you for the challenges and responsibilities you will face in your professional and personal life.

As you navigate your college sports journey, view accountability not only as an obligation but as a powerful influence that molds your character and impacts the results you attain. The power of accountability is in your hands – use it wisely and observe how it transforms your college experience.

Setting Your Personal Standard of Accountability

Now that we have explored the broader concepts of accountability, let's bring it closer to home. What does accountability personally mean to you? How can you establish your own standard of accountability to handle the special challenges of being a college athlete?

Defining Your Personal Standard

Your personal accountability standard is the framework you build for yourself. It consists of principles and commitments that steer your actions and decisions. In the world of college sports, this standard acts as your compass, guiding you through both challenging and triumphant moments.

Here are some steps to help you define your personal accountability standard:

- **Reflect on Your Values:** Consider the values that matter most to you as a college athlete. Is it integrity, discipline, or commitment? Think about the principles you want to uphold.
- **Identify Your Priorities:** In the busy life of a college student-athlete, what comes first for you? Is it academics, sports, or personal relationships? Knowing your priorities helps align your actions with your goals.
- **Set Clear Goals:** Define your aspirations as a college athlete by setting clear and achievable goals. These goals serve as markers of success and accountability.
- **Establish Daily Habits:** Accountability is a daily practice. Identify habits that contribute to your success, whether it's consistent training, completing assignments on time, or maintaining a healthy lifestyle.
- **Hold Yourself to High Standards:** Challenge yourself to aim high. Set standards that encourage you to surpass your own expectations, fostering a mindset of continuous improvement.

The Role of Self-Discipline

Self-discipline plays a crucial role in accountability. It's about staying focused on your goals, making choices that match your values, and persisting when faced with challenges. Think of self-discipline as the engine that propels your accountability forward.

Accountability on the Field/Court Defined

Let's now explore what accountability means in the context of sports. In my first year of college, following a triumphant fall season tournament, my tennis team and I were filled with much enthusiasm and joy. As we eagerly discussed plans for a celebratory dinner, we gathered around our coach. However, I sensed something wasn't right. Our coach didn't appear pleased and seemed bothered.

Coach Dash addressed the team. Despite our victories on the court, he was concerned about our on-court behavior – some teammates had displayed unsportsmanlike conduct. Coach Dash emphasized that winning was crucial but winning with integrity mattered even more. Little did I know this would be my initiation into a crucial lesson on accountability.

In college, tennis, which is primarily an individual sport, assumed a team dynamic, bringing forth numerous challenges. Coach Dash stressed that our actions reflected not only on ourselves but on the entire team and program. To drive home the importance of accountability, Coach Dash had us engage in a rigorous session of sprints, highlighting that individual accountability was paramount. Any breakdown in one member affected the entire team.

The Invisible Weapon

This direct encounter with accountability at the start of my college experience had a lasting effect, showing me the significant influence of accountability in upholding standards. Coach Dash's guidance not only influenced my performance in sports but also contributed to my personal growth. To Coach Dash, if you happen to read this, a sincere THANK YOU!

This story is more than just a recount; it's a heads-up, offering insight into a situation many athletes will face on a college team. If you haven't encountered it yet, be prepared because, believe me, it's on the horizon. College teams mirror accountability, where every action on the field or court shapes both your personal journey and the team's dynamics.

Our influence over these factors is fragile, emphasizing the need to concentrate on what we can control. One thing firmly within our grasp is accountability. It's a power that can't be enforced externally; it must radiate from within. Recognizing this early in your college experience acts as your guide for smoother navigation through these unfamiliar waters.

Let's explore the complex realm of accountability in sports. Being accountable in life sets you apart but doing so in sports thrusts you far ahead of your college peers. This often marks the first move away from parental guidance and you have to make decisions on your own. Personal accountability becomes crucial during this time period. It's your responsibility to be disciplined and make wise choices, because your coaches won't be guiding you every step of the way — they have an entire team to lead!

NOW, let's break down where accountability plays a role in sports:

1. Rest & Recovery: Make sure to take enough time to recover and be ready for practice and gameplay.

2. Nutrition: Eat the right foods to keep your body well-nourished at all times.

3. Academics: No pass, no play — academics are non-negotiable.

4. Balancing Priorities: Managing school, social life, and sports requires a delicate balance.

5. Teamwork: Strive to be the best teammate, contributing positively to the team.

6. Attitude: Maintain the right attitude through the highs, lows, and adversity.

7. Effort: Give 100%, even on days when you're not feeling 100%.

8. Upholding Team Standard: Adhere to the rules and avoid actions that could embarrass the team.

9. Upholding Personal Standard: Do what's necessary to be the best version of yourself.

The Invisible Weapon

That's quite a list, isn't it? And remember, this is just the beginning. In reality, being a college athlete involves a lot more responsibilities. You are not just a regular student; you are held to a different standard, one that is expected to be maintained throughout your college journey.

Accountability in sports goes beyond just playing; it involves the small things — the standards you uphold, your contribution to the team, and many other factors. So, take a good look at yourself.

Evaluate your accountability using the self-assessment on the following page. It's like a mirror, showing you where you stand on the accountability spectrum.

Use the blank space here to take two or three notes on what stands out to you the most and what you can do to improve in this area of accountability.

1. _____

2. _____

3. _____

ACCOUNTABILITY QUESTIONAIRRE

Answer all questions on a scale of 1-10, with 10 being the best and 1 being the worst.

How would you rate your commitment to showing up for practice on time? _____

How likely are you to take responsibility for your own mistakes during a game, without blaming external factors? _____

How often do you actively seek feedback from your coaches and teammates? _____

To what extent do you believe in your ability to meet the expectations set by your coach and team? _____

How often do you set personal goals for your performance in addition to the ones set by your coach? _____

How likely are you to maintain your fitness level and diet outside of your scheduled training hours? _____

How prepared are you to make sacrifices for your team when required, such as playing out of your preferred position? _____

How accountable do you hold yourself for your performance, regardless of the game's outcome? _____

How often do you keep practicing a skill or technique until you've mastered it, without being prompted by your coach? _____

How likely are you to persevere in your training and performance even when progress seems slow or non-existent? _____

The Invisible Weapon

Identifying areas where you may need more accountability is a positive step. Recognizing these areas is crucial for improvement. As you continue reading this chapter, pay attention to the themes and skills discussed. Use them to address and enhance the areas where you need to improve.

Impact of Accountability Beyond the Game

As you're starting to understand how accountable you are off the field or court can significantly affect how you perform on it. When I talk about accountability off the field or court, I've noticed that it can be divided into two main aspects, each with a simple solution if challenges arise.

The first main category is school. Regardless of whether you see it as a top priority or a secondary concern during your college journey, neglecting academic responsibilities can be a problem. One of the most significant pitfalls for college athletes is not taking their studies seriously, risking the privilege to play. The reality is, if you don't pass, you don't play. Committing to your studies is not only essential for playing but also for preparing yourself for life beyond sports.

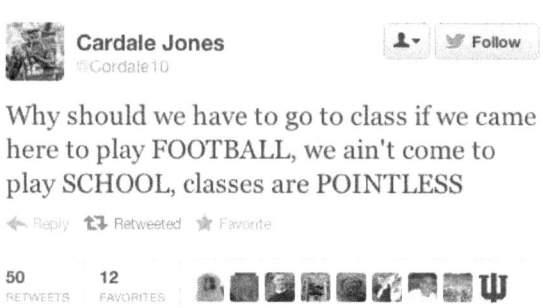

Not the greatest mindset to have as a "student"-athlete (2012)

Integrating accountability into your schoolwork can be tricky. Without your parents constantly supervising your studies, establishing discipline requires effective time management.

Here's a straightforward process:

- *Record your class schedule, study groups, and tutoring sessions.*
- *Add your practice and competition schedule, factoring in travel time.*
- *Use a calendar or a large white dry-erase board in your room.*
- *Calculate the daily hours devoted to sports and academics, prioritizing school work.*
- *Efficiently use your remaining time for studying or other academic responsibilities.*

An effective time management system provides clarity on how to make the most of your time every day.

The second main category is social life. College is undoubtedly a time for exploration, making friends, and enjoying new experiences. While this is encouraged, as a college athlete, your opportunities for socializing are limited. Late nights are not conducive to early morning workouts and practices. Balancing social life is crucial, and the key is prioritizing events. When invitations come your way, rank them by importance and assess their potential impact on your sport. Avoid events that could negatively affect your performance.

School and social life present challenges within your athletic career. The solution to staying accountable and on track is remarkably simple: MAKE THE RIGHT CHOICE. Although straightforward, making the right choices can be challenging. Human as we are, daily struggles with decision-making are inevitable. What must change is your choice-making behavior. You now have control over yourself and your actions. Consider your current and future career, and consistently make the right choices. No one else can do it for you. Don't jeopardize your commitments for momentary pleasures. Stay accountable in your academic and social life – you'll appreciate it later. The bottom line is: no pass, no play.

Effect of Accountability on the Field Performance

Being accountable in sports goes beyond the time you spend actively playing on the court or field. It includes your actions and behavior, even when you're not in the game, shaping how you navigate the world of sports beyond the actual play. The effect of accountability on your on-the-field/court performance is considerable and touches different aspects of your game. Let's explore three areas where it significantly influences your performance: consistency, resilience, and a winning mindset.

Accountability boosts performance by promoting consistency. Being consistent in training helps prevent complacency and supports steady progress toward achieving your goals. Complacency in sports can hinder your dreams. When you become complacent, you ignore crucial tasks, get too comfortable, let your guard down, lose motivation, and often take steps backward. By staying consistent in your practices, workouts, routines, and taking care of your diet and sleep, you stay on the correct path, steadily working towards your end goals.

The second crucial role of accountability plays is in developing resilience. Every athlete faces adversity in their sport. In such times, it's tempting not to give your best effort, blame others, or ignore the necessary actions to overcome difficulties. Being accountable for what you need to do when facing adversity helps you confront, tackle, and overcome challenges. It enables you to perform successfully under pressure and recover faster from setbacks. Being accountable to your practices, efforts, and discipline during tough times will help you endure and triumph over obstacles.

The third way accountability impacts performance is by cultivating a winning mindset. When you are accountable, you stay focused on your goals, whether short-term or long-term, and work towards them every single day. Additionally, it encourages determination to consistently strive for improvement. Success cannot be achieved without improvement, and accountability plays a crucial role in this process. Stay accountable, put in the work, and nurture a winning mindset.

Shaping Your Attitude for Accountability

The Invisible Weapon

In the earlier sections of this chapter, we explained what accountability truly means, exploring its complexities and basic principles. We broke down how it affects not only your sports life but also your overall success in college. Now, let's turn our attention to figuring out how you can promote accountability in both your on-the field or on-the-court activities and your life outside of sports. For a college athlete, these two aspects smoothly come together, as almost every choice beyond sports has an impact on how you perform athletically, whether in academics or social situations.

Attitude & Accountability

In both sports and life, our attitude plays a significant role in shaping and maintaining accountability. It guides how we approach each day, influences how we interact with others, determines the effort we put into tasks, and, frankly, affects various aspects of our daily lives. It's widely accepted that maintaining a positive attitude makes tasks more manageable, while a negative attitude can make even simple activities feel challenging. Our attitude not only impacts our performance on game day but also permeates every other day leading up to competitions. The good news is that your attitude is entirely 100% within your control. In both sports and life, you have the power to choose how you respond to situations, how you think about things, and how you approach your responsibilities.

Let's get real for a moment – being accountable is not easy. The daily effort required to do what's necessary to improve is a tough task. If it were simple, we'd all excel in our pursuits, and discussions like this wouldn't be necessary. Unfortunately, that's not reality. Being accountable day in and day out is hard, demanding, and sometimes frustrating. However, how we perceive accountability can make a significant difference. Instead of viewing it as a daunting and complex idea, view it as a challenge—an opportunity for personal and athletic growth. Changing your perspective is a powerful way to shape your attitude and respond positively to adversity.

When faced with a negative thought, jot it down, question it, and change it into something more positive. For example, if you think about skipping an optional 6:00 am team workout, you might initially think, "It's optional, I can skip it and work out later." Challenge this thought by asking, "Does this show a champion's mindset? Will it help me improve?" After questioning your thoughts, turn them into something motivational, like, "Attending the optional workout sets me apart from others," or "Completing the morning workout allows me a full day for study and other activities." These reframed thoughts align more positively with your growth as an athlete and an individual.

So, the next time you feel your attitude slipping when holding yourself accountable, take a moment to write down those thoughts, question them, and change them. This simple practice can turn your attitude around, providing the edge you need for that workout, game, or match, helping you stay accountable.

The Invisible Weapon
Effort & Accountability

Effort is crucial in everything we do, whether in life or sports. However, the key lies in the level of effort we choose to put in. Similar to our attitude, our effort is entirely under our control. We can choose to exert a little or go all in. Effort and accountability go hand in hand. Holding yourself accountable to specific tasks gets you started, but to truly excel, you must put in effort – MAXIMUM effort. Once you make it a habit to hold yourself accountable for giving your best in the small aspects of your sport—practices, lifts, meetings—things will start falling into place. Consistently holding yourself accountable for giving maximum effort both on and off the field or court makes you an unstoppable force.

Before we continue, let's address something about effort. On days when you feel physically and mentally sound, giving maximum effort is relatively easy and straightforward. Now, think about those days when you're tired, sore, moody, or feeling negative—it's challenging to muster your maximum effort. However, there's no excuse for not giving 100% effort every day. NONE. It has to be a full 100%. "But Coach George, if I'm tired and sore, how can I give maximum effort if I can't move like I normally do?" That's an excellent question, and this scenario arises frequently. My philosophy is to give 100% even if you aren't at 100%. If you pour everything you have into it, even if it falls short of your usual performance, that makes a difference! It's what sets you apart when you're in the midst of a game or match, giving everything you have. Providing 100% effort even when you aren't feeling 100% and holding yourself accountable to that rule will benefit you immensely in the short and long term of your college career.

So, the key is to hold yourself accountable for giving maximum effort in everything you do in life and sports, and you will begin to notice a significant change in how you operate as a student-athlete.

Creating High Standards Through Accountability

The final way to truly let accountability take effect in your life and game is by establishing a standard for yourself. A personal standard comprises rules of behavior you set to follow, shaping how you operate in life, how you approach things, and how you present yourself on and off the field or court. A personal standard is something you hold yourself accountable to every single day, reflecting who you are as a person and an athlete.

For example, here's a glimpse of my daily personal standard:

- Give 100% effort 100% of the time.
- Maintain a positive attitude when facing challenges.
- Take care of the "little things" to enable the "big things."
- Make smart choices socially; don't jeopardize what I'm working towards.
- Be disciplined and do what needs to be done, regardless of how I feel.

Your personal standard shouldn't involve specific performance outcomes. When creating your standard, steer clear of outcome-oriented objectives. These standards need to be growth-oriented — focused on the process, building for the future — to foster personal and athletic development. The standard you create should be challenging but not impossible. Now, I've provided a basic idea for creating a standard, but beyond that, it's up to you to build it and uphold it. Creating and maintaining a standard is a personal responsibility that only you can fulfill.

Conclusion

Throughout this chapter, I've highlighted how important accountability is as you start or continue your college journey. It can guide you toward success, allowing you to go beyond what you might think is possible by being responsible for the right actions and sticking to the standards you have established. I encourage you to take this chapter to heart, as I've witnessed and personally experienced the transformative power of accountability. It will undoubtedly be a game-changer in your career.

Chapter Eight: Goal Setting

*"**I**'VE LOST MY MIND DOING THIS GAME. Like Vincent Van Gogh. He dedicated his life to his art and lost his mind in the process. That's happened to me. But f**k it. When that gold belt is around my waist, when my mother has a big mansion, when my girlfriend has a different car for every day of the week, my kid's kids have anything they ever want; then it will pay. Then I'm happy, I lost my mind." - Conor McGregor*

Certainly, Conor McGregor is among the top fighters globally, only trailing my favorite, Mike Tyson. Recognized for his unwavering confidence, almost bordering on arrogance, and his remarkable skill in verbal exchanges with opponents, McGregor's real strength is evident in the octagon. McGregor has achieved a lot in his fighting career, attributing a significant part of his success to his mental prowess. McGregor boldly claims that fighting, and sports in general, is 100% mental. While physical ability is important, the core idea is that the mind holds immense control. McGregor wouldn't have reached his current level without understanding the power of the mind and, concurrently, the effectiveness of setting goals for mental and actual performance. Reflecting on his words, he expresses that he's truly dedicated his mind to pursuing his goals—a deeply impactful message. Goal setting emerges as a crucial element in achieving success in collegiate sports. Even if you're already setting goals, exploring this chapter may provide a fresh perspective and a strategic edge in how you approach goal setting.

Psychology of Goal Setting – Unveiling the Hidden Power

Setting goals, often overlooked in the sports realm, holds significant importance and numerous benefits for individual athletes and teams alike. Some athletes may underestimate its value, perhaps considering it less crucial than time spent in the gym or on the practice court. However, the reality is that dedicating time to properly set goals yields more significant long-term benefits than spending an extra twenty minutes in the gym. If there's one key takeaway from this book, let it be this: investing time to enhance your mental game is more advantageous than solely focusing on physical improvement.

Now, let's explore a few studies that shed light on the psychological and performance effects of goal setting for athletes.

In a study by Locke and Latham (2002), it was discovered that appropriately done goal setting led to a remarkable 90% improvement in performance among participants. This enhancement was attributed to the heightened motivation and focus instilled by the goal-setting process.

A remarkable 90% improvement in performance—undeniably impressive! The significant enhancements observed were connected to increased motivation and focus. As athletes and, fundamentally, as humans, our natural motivation and desire drive us toward our goals. Goal setting effectively channels and guides this motivation. Regularly reflecting on our established goals nurtures our sense of purpose, providing confidence boosts when milestones are achieved. Unless you don't enjoy accomplishing things, in which case, a revisit to Chapter Four might be in order, where motivation was discussed in detail.

Expanding on this, our inherent focus becomes powerful when aligned with the right objectives through goal setting. Keeping our "eyes on the prize" redirects our focus to the essential tasks at hand, reducing the impact of other distractions. Imagine maintaining such laser focus consistently—on the practice field/court and in competition. The potential for improved development and productivity as an athlete is profound.

Further research in sports psychology, notably by Weinberg et al. (2001), underscores the role of goal setting in reducing anxiety levels in athletes. Athletes who set performance and outcome goals experienced less pressure and stress before and during competitions, contributing to an overall improved performance.

This study brings forth interesting dynamics, especially when looking at how goal setting can reduce anxiety levels in athletes. Outcome goals can be tricky, and we'll delve into that later. For now, let's concentrate on how setting goals redirects an athlete's attention from external pressures to achieving specific objectives. Whether these goals are short-term, focused on a single game or match, or long-term, reflecting the cumulative effort over time, the shift in focus is truly transformative. Consider the difference between feeling anxious and pressured versus focusing on achievable goals tailored to the immediate or distant future. All those moments spent in pre-competition anxiety are essentially wasted, diverting focus from reaching your true potential. Acknowledge the past, embrace your humanity, and let this knowledge propel you forward.

Importance of Goal Setting in Sports
Unveiling the Recipe for Success

At this point, you might be resonating with the idea that goal setting is a fundamental recipe for development and success. Let's dive into some crucial ingredients in this recipe – the key factors that make goal setting a powerful tool.

To start, let's talk about maintaining motivation. As mentioned earlier, goal setting boosts motivation by providing a clear objective to pursue. However, goal setting isn't only about setting and achieving; it plays a crucial role in different motivational scenarios.

First, let's address the notorious "bad days." We've all been there – the days when nothing seems to go right, and your performance is subpar. In college sports, these days are almost inevitable. Goal setting steps in by offering a tool for reflection on such days. Take a moment to reflect on your objectives, how you can achieve them, and what specific actions can be taken on that challenging day to make progress toward your goals. Shifting your focus from the day's difficulties to actionable steps for improvement and goal attainment can be a game-changer during those tough practice sessions.

Now, let's flip to the opposite spectrum – the "good days"! Those days when everything clicks, you're in the zone, making plays, and thoroughly enjoying the game. Harnessing the momentum from these good days is crucial, and goal setting provides a means to do so. Reflect on your established goals on these positive days, reinforcing what you aim to accomplish and using that extra motivation to build on the momentum. It's easy to feel inspired and motivated on the good days; capitalize on that inspiration and keep your goals at the forefront for that extra spark.

Moving on, goal setting is a powerful tool for tracking progress over both short and long terms. Tracking progress is vital for building and sustaining confidence. It illuminates areas of improvement and identifies aspects that need further development. Setting both short-term and long-term goals offers a structured way to assess your progress by reaching and crossing off these objectives. This tracking mechanism provides a developmental perspective, allowing you to reassess, tweak goals, or set new ones to ensure you continue moving in the right direction.

The fourth and final area underscoring the importance of goal setting is its role in maintaining accountability and keeping you on track. Your goals serve as a guiding force, keeping you focused and accountable on a daily basis. Whether it's in the gym, on the court, or off the field, your goals set a high standard of work. Consistently staying on track is essential to realizing these goals and maintaining the level of accountability necessary for success.

In essence, goal setting isn't just a mere task to be completed; it's a dynamic process that influences your mindset, actions, and overall journey in sports. Embrace it, utilize it, and let it be your compass on the road to success.

Navigating Growth and Outcome Oriented Goals

As you learn more about goal setting, it's important to understand the two main types of goals: growth-oriented and outcome-oriented. Each serves a specific purpose, and finding the right balance between them is essential for setting goals that are both useful and achievable.

Growth-Oriented Goals: Cultivating the Growth Mindset

In alignment with the Growth Mindset, growth-oriented goals focus on continuous learning, development, and improvement. These goals highlight the journey of evolving as a player, concentrating on long-term growth rather than just winning or losing. They involve personal development, self-improvement, and intrinsic motivation.

Imagine a basketball player working to improve their free throw accuracy. The key is consistent practice and daily refinement of techniques. Similarly, a football player may set a goal to build more muscle before the season through dedicated gym work, aiming to enhance on-field performance. On the mental side, an athlete might set a goal to spend fifteen minutes each day on meditation and visualization to improve awareness on the court or field.

Growth-oriented goals highlight the importance of the journey, concentrating on daily actions that contribute to an athlete's development. By emphasizing the process over obsessing about outcomes, intrinsic motivation becomes a powerful driving force. Accomplishing growth-oriented goals is highly rewarding, signifying progress toward becoming the best version of oneself. While these goals should be a priority, it's also important to strike a balance with outcome-oriented goals for a well-rounded approach to goal setting.

Outcome Oriented Goals – Pursuing Victory

Differing from growth-oriented goals, outcome-oriented goals direct their attention outward and typically center around winning or attaining specific results or statistics in a game or match. Imagine a basketball player aiming to score five three-pointers each half, a tennis player setting a goal to win an entire weekend tournament, or a baseball pitcher working towards five strikeouts per game to enhance draft prospects after the senior season.

Outcome goals have a dual nature—they can bring both benefits and drawbacks. On the positive side, accomplishing them is incredibly satisfying, showcasing the ability to win or achieve statistical targets. However, the challenge lies in the potential for feelings of failure or unmet expectations if these goals aren't reached. Such experiences can lead to reduced confidence and motivation.

While outcome goals can be complex, they can be effective when approached with the right mindset. As you create your goals, it's vital to find a balance and use outcome-oriented goals wisely. Implement them in areas where you find them realistic and attainable, considering the potential psychological effects of achieving or not achieving them.

Goal Setting Strategies: A Blueprint for Athletic Success

In the dynamic world of sports, crafting short-term goals emerges as a potent strategy for personal growth, offering numerous advantages that can enhance your performance on the field or court. Let's explore the impactful nature of short-term goals and how to seamlessly incorporate them into your athletic journey.

1. **Focused on the Present:**

Short-term goals act as a guide for immediate objectives in both practice and competition. Imagine a basketball player committed to achieving one hundred free throws daily. This specific, daily target keeps the athlete rooted in the present, fostering continuous improvement without dwelling on the past or fixating too far into the future.

2. **Quick Sense of Accomplishment**:

Unlike their long-term counterparts, short-term goals provide a faster sense of achievement, sparking intrinsic motivation and nurturing a profound love for your sport. Envision accomplishing three short-term goals in as many weeks—the joy from each triumph fuels a desire for more success, propelling you forward and building an unstoppable momentum.

3. **Offseason Motivation:**

The offseason can be a challenging period for maintaining focus and avoiding complacency. Enter short-term goals as motivation saviors. Establishing these goals before the offseason unfolds a roadmap, ensuring you remain driven and engaged during the downtime. Consistently reaching short-term milestones becomes a game-changer, ensuring you return to the next season stronger and more refined.

The Invisible Weapon
Effective Short-Term Goal Setting:

Now, let's uncover the strategy for setting short-term goals—a three-step process crafted to enhance your growth as a player.

Step One: Reflect and Recognize:

Take a moment to think about your game. Identify areas that call for improvement in the short term. Recognizing these specifics is the initial step toward meaningful progress.

Step Two: Precision in Improvement:

Once you've acknowledged areas for enhancement, create specific strategies to refine your skills. Make your short-term goals clear, specific, and measurable. Vague goals can lead to confusion and a lack of direction. For example, if your tennis serve needs improvement, concentrate on enhancing first serve consistency. Dedicate time each day to focused practice sessions, aiming for a concrete goal, such as achieving over 80% accuracy in twenty serves.

Step Three: Set a Realistic Timetable:

Establish a reasonable timeframe to achieve your goal. If challenges arise, don't be disheartened—adjust your timeline. Progress takes time in sports, and setbacks are part of the journey. Stay persistent, and success will inevitably follow.

In conclusion, the significance of short-term goals in sports and player development cannot be overstated. Start today. List your goals. Conquer them. Your journey to greatness begins with these incremental victories.

Strategies for Long-Term Goals

Exploring the realm of long-term goals, a distinctive aspect in the landscape of achievement, demands careful attention and a strategic approach. In this chapter, we delve into the unique benefits that long-term goals bring to your game and how to shape them for enduring success.

1. **Beyond Wins and Losses:**
    - Long-term goals provide athletes with guidance beyond the simple dichotomy of winning or losing. Assessing a season goes beyond counting victories; it involves gauging growth and improvement over time. Embracing growth-oriented long-term goals ensures that your journey is not solely determined by the scoreboard but by the developmental milestones you achieve. The satisfaction of reaching these goals acts as potent momentum, propelling you into the offseason or concluding the season on a resounding note.
2. **Resilience in Tough Times:**
    - During adversity, facing a series of challenging losses, or not performing at your peak, long-term

goals act as a compass. Reflecting on your overarching purpose as an athlete, grounded in these goals, helps recalibrate your focus. It shifts your attention from immediate struggles to the enduring pursuit of improvement. Instead of being consumed by present difficulties, you remain steadfast on the path toward a brighter athletic future.

3. **A Sense of Direction:**
   - Long-term goals provide a roadmap for athletes, preventing them from wandering aimlessly in their sporting journey. Without a clear vision of what they want to achieve, athletes risk floundering in their pursuits. Long-term goals serve as guideposts, offering clarity and direction. Whether it's your college career or the broader scope of your athletic endeavors, these goals help articulate and refine your aspirations.

Creating long-term goals for your athletic growth is super important. Here's a simple guide to help you make goals that are achievable and focused on getting better.

Step One: Imagine Your Future

Think about yourself in six months, a year, or at the end of the sports season. Picture how you want to play and improve. Imagine becoming a better version of yourself but keep it realistic.

Step Two: Find a Balance Between Growth and Outcome

Write down the things you want and separate them into goals for getting better and goals for achieving specific results. Try to have a mix but lean more towards getting better. Make sure your goals make sense and write them down to show you're serious.

Step Three: Work Together for Success

Talk to yourself, your coaches, and your teammates about your goals. Figure out steps you can take on and off the field, in the gym, or wherever you practice. Working together makes your plan stronger and helps you have a better chance of reaching your long-term goals.

Step Four: Commit and Set a Timeline

Once you know your goals and have a plan, decide on a realistic time to achieve them. Promise yourself to stick to this plan, knowing that progress happens slowly. Being committed is the key to succeeding in the long run. Start your journey with these simple steps for making long-term goals. See how your path in sports becomes clearer and more purposeful.

Conclusion

This chapter has helped you learn about setting goals. As you go ahead, feel confident and find it easier to set your goals. Whether you're planning for big achievements in the long run or smaller successes in the short term, it's important to balance goals that help you grow with those that focus on results. This is your moment to invest in yourself, set big goals, and then work hard to

The Invisible Weapon

make them happen! Success is waiting for you – go after it with determination and purpose!

Chapter Nine: Performance Anxiety

"I'M A COUPLE HOURS AWAY from the biggest match of my career. The biggest match of my life. I was just curled up in a ball, trying desperately to figure out a way to just stop having these thoughts. And I'm about to play the greatest player of all time…to get into the quarterfinals of the US Open. This match, I had physically and mentally and emotionally trained for my entire life. And now, in the car ride to Arthur Ashe Stadium, my mind is a million places. All of a sudden, just…BOOM! The thoughts just came flooding in, more and more and more. Just nonstop thoughts. And my heart is just racing. Big, deep breaths. I'm Googling "what is anxiety disorder", "panic disorder," "mental health." I'm listening to talks on YouTube of how to deal with it, how to beat it, thinking, "How am I gonna get through this?". I mean, just basically, I'm…I'm desperate. I didn't know what to do." - Mardy Fish

The Invisible Weapon

> *Disclaimer: This book chapter includes discussion of mental health topics. It is intended to provide general information and understanding about mental health and should not be used in place of professional advice from a qualified healthcare provider. If you are struggling with mental health issues, please seek professional help. If you are experiencing a mental health crisis, please contact a crisis hotline. I am not a licensed counselor/psychologist, and the advice in this chapter does not provide professional psychological advice or treatment.*

"I'm a couple of hours away from the biggest match of my career. The biggest match of my life." These words from Mardy Fish capture the intense reality of performance anxiety, a struggle that affects even the most elite athletes. As he geared up to compete against Roger Federer at the US Open, the gravity of the moment triggered a storm of thoughts and emotions.

Imagine it: a mind racing with thoughts, a pounding heart, beads of sweat forming, and a stomach tied in knots. It's a combination of symptoms that anyone who has confronted a daunting match or game can understand. Mardy Fish's experience highlights how common performance anxiety is in the world of sports. You might have experienced a fraction of what he described – anxiety appearing just before a crucial moment.

Mardy Fish, a seasoned tennis player, enjoyed a remarkable career marked by a hidden struggle with performance anxiety. Although not openly discussed during his playing days, he contended with this challenge for a significant part of his professional career. His struggle extended beyond the confines of the court, weaving into aspects of his personal life. As repeatedly highlighted in this book, this underscores the extensive impact of anxiety on various aspects of an athlete's life.

By sharing his experiences, Fish brings attention to how anxiety impacts both an athlete's performance and their personal life. His story serves as a powerful reminder that athletes, regardless of their skill level, deal with these challenges. His willingness to discuss these challenges publicly not only recounts a personal journey but also creates a space to break the stigma surrounding the often-unspoken battles that athletes face.

Performance anxiety doesn't discriminate. It accompanies athletes at every stage of their journey, whether they are just beginning or reaching the pinnacle of their sport. Mardy Fish's story emphasizes that acknowledging these feelings is the first step. It's acceptable to feel the pressure, the worry, the panic. What matters is how you respond in those moments to overcome anxiety and to shift your focus.

As we delve into the complexities of performance anxiety in this chapter, remember it's a shared struggle. Mardy Fish's journey is a beacon of courage, inviting athletes at every level to recognize, confront, and conquer the challenges that come with the territory.

Understanding Anxiety

Before exploring the details of performance anxiety in sports, let's expand our understanding of anxiety beyond the athletic arena.

The Invisible Weapon

Anxiety, as an emotion, shows up as feelings of tension, worrisome thoughts, and physical changes such as increased blood pressure. Those dealing with anxiety often contend with repetitive intrusive thoughts, avoid situations due to worry or apprehension, and experience physical symptoms like sweating, trembling, dizziness and rapid heartbeat.

It's important to distinguish anxiety from fear, even though they're often considered together. Anxiety is a response that looks ahead, lasting longer, and aims to manage a potential threat. On the other hand, fear is a response focused on the present, brief, and linked to a clearly identifiable and specific threat. In simple terms, anxiety is how we react to real or imagined situations or challenges, whether they are happening now or in the future. It's normal for people to handle anxiety differently because we're all wired in unique ways.

The impact of anxiety extends beyond the mind, affecting the body over prolonged periods. Anxiety triggers the release of stress hormones, resulting in a perpetually uptight and tense body, and a mind racing at full speed. Additionally, it can cause the hypothalamus, responsible for emotional responses, to shrink, impacting learning, memory, and emotional control. Furthermore, anxiety activates the body's fight or flight response, flooding the bloodstream with adrenaline and cortisol. This constant flow, without relaxation and recovery, can lead to sustained periods of heightened stress.

As a college athlete, it's evident that anxiety plays a significant role in our daily lives and, crucially, in our athletic performance. To gauge the potential presence of anxiety in your life, consider completing the GAD-7 (Generalized Anxiety Disorder) questionnaire provided below. Understanding and addressing anxiety is a vital step in optimizing both your mental and physical well-being.

GAD-7

Over the last 2 weeks, how often have you been bothered by the following problems?	Not at all	Several days	More than half the days	Nearly every day
1. Feeling nervous, anxious or on edge	0	1	2	3
2. Not being able to stop or control worrying	0	1	2	3
3. Worrying too much about different things	0	1	2	3
4. Trouble relaxing	0	1	2	3
5. Being so restless that it is hard to sit still	0	1	2	3
6. Becoming easily annoyed or irritable	0	1	2	3
7. Feeling afraid as if something awful might happen	0	1	2	3

Total Score ___ = Add Columns ___ + ___ + ___

If you checked off any problems, how difficult have these problems made it for you to do your work, take care of things at home, or get along with other people?

Not difficult at all	Somewhat difficult	Very difficult	Extremely difficult
☐	☐	☐	☐

Understanding Performance Anxiety

Before we address performance anxiety directly, it's important to unravel its complexities and comprehend the various reasons that impact athletes. Just like our diverse skill sets, our brains are wired uniquely, resulting in different things that set off anxiety and how we react to them. Anxiety, a common emotion, can be triggered by a variety of factors, and in the sports world, these triggers are varied and personal.

Identifying seven common causes of anxiety in athletes lays the groundwork for our exploration:

1. **High Expectations:** Feeling pressure to meet personal or external expectations can cause anxiety, as there is the fear of disappointing oneself, coaches, or fans.
2. **Fear of Failure:** Anxiety may arise from the fear of failing and the potential consequences, such as loss of status, self-esteem, or disappointment from others.
3. **Past Experiences:** Negative memories from previous sports performances can linger, inducing anxiety about repeating mistakes or underperforming.
4. **Injury Worries:** Apprehension about physical injury, especially for athletes with a history of significant injuries or surgeries, can contribute to performance anxiety.
5. **Lack of Preparation:** Feeling unprepared due to inadequate training, poor nutrition, or insufficient rest and recovery can heighten anxiety levels.
6. **Public Scrutiny:** The constant public spotlight can cause stress and anxiety, as athletes feel scrutinized both on and off the field/court, especially at the college level.

7. **Overemphasis on Results:** A focus primarily on outcomes rather than the process can result in stress and anxiety about winning or losing.

Recognizing the mental effects of anxiety is crucial because they can directly affect performance. Some significant ways anxiety can impact your performance include:

1. **Increased Stress and Tension:** Feeling overwhelming stress or tension can disrupt concentration and hinder optimal athletic performance.
2. **Fear of Failure:** Intense fear can immobilize athletes, preventing them from performing well or participating altogether.
3. **Poor Concentration:** Anxious thoughts can result in poor focus and concentration during crucial moments.
4. **Decreased Self-esteem and Confidence:** Anxiety-induced feelings of inadequacy can wear down an athlete's self-confidence.

Understanding the physical effects of anxiety is equally important:

1. **Increased Heart Rate and Blood Pressure:** Uncomfortable symptoms that can hinder an athlete's performance.
2. **Muscle Tension and Shaking:** Involuntary muscle reactions that impede an athlete's ability to perform.
3. **Dry Mouth and Throat:** Discomfort that can affect speech and swallowing.

4. **Shortness of Breath or Hyperventilation:** Symptoms that limit endurance and physical capabilities.

Understanding that performance anxiety is a natural aspect of an athlete's journey is the initial step. The positive news is that there are strategies available to reduce its impact. Developing the ability to identify and address anxiety will distinguish you in the college sports world, where mastering anxiety management becomes a valuable skill. While anxiety is a basic human reaction, becoming skilled at managing it is one of the more challenging aspects of athletic life.

Conquering Anxiety

Now that you've got a solid grasp of performance anxiety, and if it's making you a bit uneasy, don't worry—there are solutions! This section focuses on addressing the physical and mental impact of anxiety on your game. The tools of choice? Two straightforward yet powerful skills: deep breathing and PMR (Progressive Muscle Relaxation).

While these techniques might seem simple (after all, we've been breathing and stretching our whole lives), the real question is whether you've been doing them correctly and in ways that can genuinely improve your performance. Let's explore the transformative potential of combining deep breathing and PMR. This powerful duo has the potential to be a game-changer in your efforts to overcome the effects of performance anxiety.

Coping with Anxiety Effect
Mastering Deep Breathing Techniques

Deep breathing serves as a remedy for both mental and physical effects of anxiety. Despite its simplicity, it packs a punch in effectiveness. This technique acts as a powerful tool against anxiety symptoms, such as shortness of breath, a racing heart, poor concentration, and stress. The key lies in triggering the body's natural relaxation response – slowing the heart rate, lowering blood pressure, gaining control over breathing, and counteracting the stress response.

Here's a simple deep breathing technique:

1. Get into a comfortable position, whether sitting or lying down.

2. Place one hand on your chest and the other on your stomach.

3. Inhale slowly through your nose for four seconds: Feel your lungs fill with air.

4. Hold your breath for two seconds.

5. Exhale slowly through your mouth for six seconds. Feel relaxation with each breath out.

6. Repeat for several rounds or until you feel relaxed.

The Invisible Weapon

Incorporate this simple deep breathing routine before a game or match or when you start feeling anxious. Moreover, practice deep breathing during calm moments to make it a habit. This enhances overall relaxation and equips you to manage stress responses effectively.

Take it a step further with the "box method" or "circle method." Concentrating on a visual representation of a box or circle while deep breathing shifts your focus away from anxiety and fear temporarily. Spend 10-15 seconds inhaling along the perimeter and exhaling as you complete the shape. Whether focusing on a physical object or visualizing it with closed eyes, both approaches have their merits – keeping you present or momentarily disconnecting you from your surroundings.

You can also refer back to the larger box breathing diagram from page 62.

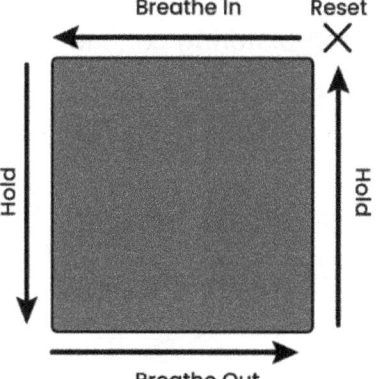

Highlighting the importance of effective breathing when you feel pressured is crucial. Inhaling and exhaling, especially during box/circle breathing, helps bring your body into balance, acting as a mental anchor. Even basic deep breathing can be highly effective—

regaining control over your rhythm allows for a reset and clear thinking. Intentionally focusing on your breath minimizes wandering thoughts, providing greater control during stressful situations or before a challenging match or game.

Combating Anxiety Effects
Progressive Muscle Relaxation (PMR)

Progressive Muscle Relaxation (PMR) stands as a widely recognized technique utilized in counseling and sports settings. PMR entails systematically tensing and then relaxing different muscle groups in conjunction with deep breathing. The primary objective is to heighten awareness and differentiate between feelings of tension and relaxation. As the body progressively relaxes, tension and tightness dissipate, subsequently alleviating stress and anxiety. Consistent practice enhances overall relaxation and mental clarity, making PMR a valuable tool for mitigating performance anxiety and bolstering confidence.

Now, let's explore a simple self-guided PMR exercise to help you get started:

Guided Instructions

Step 1: Find a Comfortable Spot

Select a quiet, comfortable place where you won't be interrupted. Sit or lie down, ensuring your body is fully supported and relaxed.

Step 2: Close Your Eyes

Gently close your eyes and take a few deep breaths. Inhale through your nose for four counts, hold for four counts, then exhale through your mouth for eight counts.

Step 3: Foot Muscle Group

Start with your toes. Curl them tightly for 5 seconds, feeling the tension. After holding, abruptly release all tension and let your toes relax. Notice the sensation of relief that comes from letting go.

Step 4: Lower Leg Muscle Group

Next, focus on your calf muscles. Pull your toes towards your face to tense these muscles. Hold for 5 seconds, then relax.

Step 5: Upper Leg Muscle Group

Tighten your thighs by pressing your knees together as hard as you can for 5 seconds, then relax.

Step 6: Hips and Buttocks

Tense the muscles of your hips and buttocks. Hold for 5 seconds, then relax, feeling the tension melting away.

Step 7: Stomach

Tighten your stomach muscles. Hold for 5 seconds, then release.

Step 8: Arms

Make fists and tighten your biceps. After 5 seconds, release and gently extend your fingers and arms. Do the same as you tighten and release your triceps muscles. Do the same as you tighten and release your forearms.

Step 9: Shoulders and Neck

Pull your shoulders towards your ears to tense your neck and shoulders. Hold for 5 seconds, then relax.

Step 10: Face

Finally, tighten the muscles in your face by squeezing your eyes shut and clenching your jaw. After holding this for 5 seconds, completely relax.

After going through all muscle groups, take a few moments to enjoy the feeling of relaxation. With regular practice, this technique can help athletes manage stress and improve overall performance. Feel free to customize and fine-tune this exercise to suit your preferences, allowing you to target specific muscle groups. The beauty of this workout lies in its flexibility and adaptability to your unique needs. Take the time to discover what truly works best for you!

    Practicing PMR is beneficial for entering a focused state before a competition or calming down and regaining focus before a significant event. Consistent practice enhances your awareness, promoting a relaxed state that counteracts performance anxiety and results in better competition performances. Integrate PMR into your daily routine, and you'll observe positive changes over time.

Overcoming Performance Anxiety
Transforming the Mindset

At the start of this chapter, we explored seven fundamental areas universally contributing to performance anxiety among college athletes. Let's dig into each of these causes and understand how reshaping the mindset can effectively combat performance anxiety, unlocking your mind's potential for optimal performance.

High Expectations: While high expectations can be motivating, they can also be detrimental to mental well-being. Reframe expectations by shifting the focus from results to the process. Concentrate on giving your best, enjoy each moment, and focus on continuous improvement. Prioritize growth over mere wins and losses to significantly alleviate performance anxiety.

Fear of Failure: Fear of failure is a common concern for athletes, driven not by the act of failing but by the potential consequences of failure. Combat this fear by concentrating on the process rather than fixating on the outcome. Focus on what you can control. Focus on the present. Embrace each game or practice as an opportunity to learn and grow. Mistakes should be seen as stepping stones to improvement, not as embarrassing failures.

Past Experiences: Lingering on past experiences can be paralyzing. Past experiences are exactly that – THE PAST. Combat this cognitive hurdle by acknowledging that the past is unchangeable. Focus on the present, take deep breaths, and remind yourself that lessons from past experiences have better prepared you for future challenges.

Injury Worries: The fear of re-injury or physical pain is prevalent, especially after significant injuries. Counter these worries by ensuring thorough preparation. Focus on your current level of preparation. Regular training, appropriate exercises, and consultations with coaches or trainers can instill confidence and reduce anxiety about potential injuries.

Lack of Preparation: Feeling unprepared before a game can overwhelm the mind. Prioritize rest, recovery, and nutrition to address controllable elements of preparation. Make wise off-field/court choices, maintaining a balance that won't affect your performance negatively. By ensuring these aspects, you can boost your confidence and minimize performance anxiety.

Public Scrutiny: College athletes are constantly under public scrutiny, facing judgments and opinions. Tune out external noise and focus on what you can control: your attitude, effort, and preparation. Others' opinions should not sway your self-perception when they are not in your shoes, doing what you do every time you step onto the field or court.

Overemphasis on Results: This is IMPORTANT. Shift your focus from obsessing over results to prioritizing the process. Concentrate on your strengths, controllables, and personal development as a player. Playing to improve rather than just to win can alleviate the anxious pressure associated with outcome-focused thinking.

Conclusion New Focus

After reading this chapter. mastering the skill of overcoming performance anxiety should be your top priority. Whether it's a constant struggle or an occasional challenge, knowing how to handle performance anxiety is essential for consistent peak performance. Take proactive steps, be prepared, and, most importantly, be ready to tackle it head-on!

Chapter Ten: Mental Health and Recovery

As I STARTED WRITING this book, my aim was straightforward: to provide advice for college athletes, both present and future, connecting the realms of sports and personal development. Using my own experiences as a player, coach, and mental coach, I've seen how mental health can significantly influence athletes' lives, going beyond just performance worries.

Navigating the Challenges: My Personal Journey

As a college athlete, I faced challenges, stress, and anxiety that were more significant than I had ever anticipated. Despite the common perception of college as a time of enjoyment, I encountered unique pressures, particularly as an athlete. Managing academics, sports, and a social life proved to be overwhelming. The distinct responsibilities and demands placed on college athletes meant that neglecting one area often affected the others. I struggled with mental health issues, especially in trying to find a balance. Juggling academics and tennis sometimes took a toll on my mental well-being, worsened by misguided attempts to fit in with the stereotypical college experience. Like many athletes, I initially lacked awareness of the available resources for mental health support.

A Coach's Perspective: Unveiling the Hidden Struggles

Shifting from being a player to a coach gave me a broader view of mental health in college athletics. Coaches observe the various mental states of their players, affecting both performance and overall well-being. While some athletes handle these challenges well, others struggle with mental health throughout their college years. The frustration and sadness resulting from these struggles are evident, and as a coach, I felt the limitations of my role in addressing these issues.

During my coaching years, I pursued a Master's degree in Clinical and Mental Health Counseling, with a focus on Sports Psychology. My journey involved hands-on training at university counseling centers through practicum and internship experiences. Counseling student-athletes provided a unique understanding of how mental health profoundly influences their college experiences. Witnessing this impact fueled my passion for raising awareness about mental health and supporting athletes through difficult times.

Mental Health in College Athletics: A Crucial Focus

The mental well-being of athletes has a big impact on their time as players and their overall college journey. Despite more focus on mental health in sports in recent times, there's still a stigma attached. Athletes, afraid of negative consequences like being seen as a "problem" or someone who can't "handle the pressure," may avoid seeking help. It's crucial to recognize that facing mental health challenges is a common part of life. College athletes, with their unique lifestyle and pressures, are especially likely to deal with these difficulties.

Alarming Statistics on Mental Health in College Sports

Research indicates alarming rates of mental health challenges among college athletes. A survey by the NCAA revealed that approximately 30% of student-athletes reported overwhelming anxiety, with 25% grappling with serious depression. Gender disparities were evident, with 38% of women athletes experiencing debilitating anxiety and 28% facing severe depression.[3] Substance abuse, closely linked to mental health, is also prevalent among athletes, with higher reported rates compared to non-athletes.

It's Okay to Not Feel Okay: Embracing the Reality

"It's okay not to feel okay." Take a moment to think about this statement. Understanding that facing mental health challenges is normal is an important starting point. Athletes, who are usually in tune with their physical well-being, may find it challenging to deal with mental health issues. Unlike physical injuries that have more

---

[3] [^3^]: NCAA. "Mental Health Statistics among Student-Athletes". NCAA Student-Athlete Mental Health Survey (DATE TO BE INSERTED). https://www.ncaa.org/sites/default/files/2019RES_National_SEMHS_PublicReport_20190404.pdf

visible signs, mental health concerns can leave athletes unsure about where to seek support. Breaking the stigma around mental health is crucial, encouraging athletes to reach out for help and prioritize their overall well-being.

Finding Resources: A Path to Recovery

For athletes hesitant to approach their university counseling centers due to concerns about anonymity, alternative resources exist. The Jed Foundation and the NCAA's dedicated mental health resources provide valuable support. Recognizing that seeking help is a sign of strength, not weakness, is essential for athletes navigating mental health challenges.

Recovery: A Holistic Approach

Recovery goes beyond physical actions like stretching and ice baths, and recognizing the significance of mental recovery is crucial.

Taking care of your mind is crucial in the midst of college sports chaos, and two key practices can help. Reflecting on your day allows you to decompress and gain perspective. Focus on positive aspects to reinforce a good mindset. Another important practice is incorporating "self-care" into your daily routine—dedicating time to activities that bring joy and relaxation, providing a mental break from the pressures of sports, academics, and social life.

When it comes to physical recovery, quality sleep is a powerful tool, aiming for seven to nine hours each night. Even short naps can recharge your body. Pay attention to your nutrition to support your body's recovery.

Conclusion: Unleashing the Power of the Mind

This book has given you a toolkit for sports psychology, emphasizing the importance of sharpening your most powerful tool—your mind. The valuable insights and tools shared are sometimes ignored by college athletes. Now, the task is to turn this knowledge into action. Don't postpone it; take early steps to cultivate your mind along with your body. Keep in mind that the mind guides the body, and your most precious weapon is ready for your direction.

About the Author

George is a trained Mental Coach with a background in sports, psychology, and counseling. He began his journey at Tyler Junior College, earning an Associate's degree in Psychology and All-American honors in tennis. George then pursued a Psychology degree at Indiana University, competing in Division 1 tennis. He completed his Master's Degree in Clinical and Mental Health Counseling from UT San Antonio, also serving as an assistant coach at Trinity University (NCAA Division 3). With seven years of collegiate coaching experience, George has guided multiple All-Americans and achieved top national rankings. His personal mission is to develop outstanding athletes and individuals. George lives in Houston with his two beagles, enjoying time with family and friends.

If this book has moved or impacted you, reach out!

George@hmperform.com

IG: @Grivers4 or @hm_perform

www.hmperform.com

www.ingramcontent.com/pod-product-compliance
Lightning Source LLC
LaVergne TN
LVHW041625070426
835507LV00008B/459